The Church
Round the Corner

by

Maurice Packham

QUEENSPARK BOOK 38

To Jumbo

Contents

'If the people at St Anne's knew what a wicked boy
you are, they wouldn't come to church.'

foreworò

Redundant is the sentence passed on many churches to-day. Some are pulled down and others adapted for secular use. These are usually Victorian churches built at a time when Sunday worship was the pattern rather than the exception. St Anne's, Burlington Street, Brighton was a lovely little Victorian Gothic church and I have tried to recall some of the parishioners, the choir, social activities and the two dominant personalities: Canon T J James and the choirmaster, G H Witcombe.

Maurice Packham, Horsham, 1998

New Every Morning
1935

Sunday morning bell and mother in a fluster. 'Aren't you ready yet? Give those shoes a polish: I'm not having you show me up in front of the Old Girls.' Today will be a scorcher, and my brother, ten years my senior, won't be going to church. Very soon he'll be down on Brighton beach, launching his canoe into the placid waters. He'll take the portable Decca with the latest record *Stormy Weather* and lie stretched out on a towel under a blazing sky. Mother who has the Sunday roast to prepare, a ritual as inviolable as any of the Thirty Nine Articles, will be going this evening, best-hatted, punishing shoes and a Sunday frock from her meagre wardrobe. 'Look at your face!' she cries, demanding a physical impossibility; 'and your knees are filthy.' So, scrubbed, shining in unaccustomed Sunday finery and in a faint odour of sanctity, I make my way up Bristol Road towards St Anne's Church.

Sunday morning bell, and the summer sunshine flooding through the 'West' window, for St Anne's Church, like many others in Brighton including St Peter's the Parish Church, is aligned north and south. The sidesmen are ready at the door to give out hymn books, prayer books, greetings, commiserations and congratulations as necessary; while in the vestry, early arriving book boys open the music cupboard and take out folders containing the chosen Te Deum, Jubilate and anthem. Be-cassocked and solemn they enter the chancel and distribute the music and hymn lists along the choir desks, then collect the hymn books in readiness for the procession. Tozzer Witcombe the choirmaster arrives, clustered round with boys whose noisy chatter and laughter he quells with a frown and raised finger. But they bubble up again as they take down their cassocks from the pegs, recounting the week's events: schoolmaster injustices, schoolboy tricks, schoolboy jokes, 'Did you Hears' and 'Have you Heards'.

Sunday morning bell and the choirmen arrive, and one complains that somebody has taken his cassock and the one left on his peg is too short in the arm and half-way up his legs. If it happens again, he'll walk out. He rummages through the other cassocks, eventually finding his own. The boys reach down their Eton collars from the shelf: stiff, uncomfortable things with a made-up black bow which snaps into a stud. Some are grubbier and limper than others, matching the wearers, while those of the new boys are of pristine shininess. A choirman takes a boy by the shoulder and brushes his hair fiercely with a brush that must have hung by the vestry mirror since before the Great War. A wag quips: 'You won't have to do that in Heaven: no more partings up there.' Groans and a ripple of laughter cross the vestry and out comes Tozzer from the Vicar's side to remind the boys that they are in God's House not a bear garden.

Sunday morning bell and the street door clicks open and in bounces Jumbo, more formally known as The Canon, smiling affably and waving a greeting to nobody in particular and everybody in general. He joins Tozzer and his voice booms over the dividing partition. Whether from the pulpit or across the street, Jumbo addresses the world double forte coloured with a touch of Welsh. They are now joined by the Vicar's Warden, Mr Forward, gravitas epitomised, who has come for the slips of paper giving chapter and verse of the two morning lessons. He will read the first from the Old Testament, and Sir Hubert Bond the second from the New. At the lectern he turns over the pages of the Bible and inserts the slips in the right places.

The bell stops, and anon Mr Chatfield the rope puller and local watchmaker enters the vestry. 'How's the tempus?' booms Jumbo, now ready in his cassock, surplice and stole and the Time Expert says five minutes to go. Tozzer also be-cassocked and in his sleeveless organist's surplice, which allows freedom of arm movement, now enters the chancel, bows at the altar, crosses to the organ and switches on the blower. He waits for the bellows to inflate, flexes his fingers and soon the church fills with Sunday morning music. Back in the vestry the choir lines up behind the door, hymn books open, awaiting the opening prayer. Top boy Phillip Jarman ticks off a chorister for chewing, and a late boy dashes in, red faced and perspiring, and changes rapidly into cassock and surplice under reproachful eyes.

The church is filling now with ladies in floral frocks, best Sunday summer hats and elbow-length gloves; and some of the gentlemen wear alpaca jackets. There is a subdued garden party atmosphere. The ladies turn in their seats to chat with friends, smothering smiles behind white gloves, while older ladies in darker clothing of an earlier period sit bolt upright, black gloved under black glazed hats, half turning with a frown at the unseemly chatter. The Vicar and People's Wardens take their places on either side of the main aisle by their wands of office. Although the days of rented pews have long since passed, and the little brass frames into which cards were once slid are now empty, a territorial exclusiveness still lingers. Who would dare to sit in Lady Baddeley's accustomed pew? Mrs Marsh the Greengrocer would glare like thunder at anybody usurping *her* place.

In his mirror Tozzer has seen Chatfield the Crucifer leading the choir out from the vestry, and modulates into a key ready for the processional hymn. Now the congregation stands, and the choir moves through the chancel gates, bowing in turn at the altar and dividing like square dancers in slow motion to fill the Cantoris and Decani sides. The morning service has begun.

* * * * *

From a distance of over sixty years, memory plays tricks, retouches the picture and even adds details to the original; but the colour that Sunday morning is still fresh. The music, the canticles, psalms and anthem are not distant echoes, and I can hear the voice of the Vicar's Warden reading the lesson.

My ears were sharp in those days, so I don't think I am mistaken in thinking that Mr Forward used to pronounce 'whoremonger' as 'warmonger'. I suppose in the 30s, with the distant rumble of approaching conflict, the latter was a much used word, but I rather gather he baulked at reading the good old Anglo Saxon term for fear of shocking the Old Girls. Sir Hubert Bond, who read the second lesson, was a dapper, neatly dressed medico with a goatee beard, and I expect he would have discussed ailments of the urinary tract with anybody, anywhere, without turning a hair. Mr Forward on the other hand was a Chief Inspector of Police with a well-developed sense of propriety.

The psalms have always been my especial delight: the freshness and clarity of the 1611 version are a joy. But, when as a choirboy I peeped through the chancel railings, I wondered if they were entirely appropriate for a twentieth-century, urban congregation. There was Mrs Collyer singing 'I will offer bullocks with goats' as lustily as the rest, but the thought of her and the other ladies slitting throats with sacrificial knives, their summer frocks drenched with steaming blood was bizarre to say the least. And I wonder if it ever crossed their minds to enquire who exactly Og the King of Bashan was.

Canon James's sermons were not deeply theological discourses and seldom, I regret to say, very riveting. They were full of wise saws and modern instances and once, I remember, about a parcel of chops somebody had dropped just outside the vestry door, providing a homily on Waste. The Younger Generation came in for a lot of stick. He seemed to have forgotten that the war in which he won his MC was fought by young men of eighteen and in their twenties; although he could be forgiven for not knowing that the same age group would, in a few years, be engaged in another struggle. He never reached a peroration - or rather he almost reached one several times. Just when you hoped the sermon was coming to a close, he would be reminded of something else. I suppose you could call this the Arabian Nights Syndrome, though Scheherezade wouldn't have survived the first night if she'd been half as dull. Michael McVittie, who was a chorister at St Anne's, assured me that Tozzer had an uncanny knack of sensing when Jumbo was coming to a close and would switch on the organ blower ready for the last hymn. But I rather think it was the choirmaster's way of hinting that the sermon had gone on long enough.

And then the organ voluntary, that glorious burst of triumphant music: the only public performance I know of in which the audience gets up in a body and walks out. The service over, now begins the happy gossip and exchange of pleasantries as the congregation slowly makes its way down the aisles to the porch, where Jumbo awaits for the handshake ritual. The Old Girls slacken to a snail's pace nearer the porch, fearful of missing that handshake and being denied a word or two with him. Hurry, and you'll have to pass him by while he chats to Mrs Lynn about the church linen, or lingers overlong with Lady Baddeley, whom he wants to open the bazaar. Jumbo has long ago developed the regal technique of making each one feel special, and yet dismissing them gracefully for the next handshake.

Garbs of holiness now discarded and hung on pegs, the choristers become boys again, and released into Burlington

Street they give vent to the pent-up energy of the last hour. Tozzer emerges and ticks off an over-boisterous child who appears to be twisting a smaller boy's arm off. An iron gate to a narrow passage behind the church groans open as an elderly choirman makes his urgent way to the lavatory at the back. The summer sun blazes down, but the choirboys' afternoon will not be free. They will be required to sing at the children's service. I make my way home.

On the stairs I smell roast beef; and soon, on the dinner table there will be roast potatoes as well, greens, peas and a Yorkshire pudding cooked in the traditional fashion. None of your little round cakes, dry as a bone inside. Mother's Yorkshire was a great slab in a rectangular tin, crisp outside and deliciously soft within.

Childhood and Church

Before the church was demolished in 1986 interior photographs were taken, including one of the ornate Victorian font. Round this, in March 1925 stood my christening party: my brother, aged ten, probably playing up as usual for he was a restless, mischievous child, my mother and aunts including my favourite, Cissy, who acted as godmother. My father had died some five months earlier.

Left widowed, my mother, like many other housewives of that time, had no professional training apart from what she had learnt in service as a girl, so she got down on her knees and scrubbed floors. When she was first employed as church cleaner at St Anne's I do not know, but ever since I could crawl I followed her round the pews on a Saturday morning, she armed with mop and bucket and always wearing a hat, complying with the chauvinistic dictate of St Paul. Whether the Old Girls of the church were genuinely sympathetic towards a fatherless child and his widowed mother, or merely being patronising I shall never know now; but generally speaking they were kindly disposed. Poor soul, was the attitude, she works hard to pay the rent and keep her two boys fed and clothed. She deserves our sympathy. She was also a soft touch when it came to scrubbing floors for a pittance, taking on jobs all over Kemp Town when threepence an hour was considered generous. Perhaps the Old Girls thought they were doing her a favour, so we shouldn't be too hard on them. I always remember my mother's hands: deeply etched and criss-crossed with the evidence of hard labour. A palmist would have no problem telling her fortune, past, present or future. 'I must get my hands right,' she used to say ruefully; but she never did. The evidence of a hard life remained on her hands until her death at the age of 91. It has often crossed my mind that St Peter should line up new arrivals and ask for a hand inspection, rejecting all those whose hands were soft and milky.

Well into her eighties my mother always referred to the flower arrangers, polishers of brasswork with their gloves, tins of Bluebell and chamois leathers, and all the others fussing about and doing nothing in particular as The Old Girls Round the Church. 'Flowers may be sent to Mrs James, the Vicar's wife' was the notice in the parish magazine. This was the arrangement right up until the poor lady was senile;

a kindness of her husband who didn't want her left out. She was a fragile little creature with a very clumsy deaf aid of the period, which she wore on her chest. She always had a kind smile. Their wedding must have been a sumptuous affair held in the Royal Pavilion, Brighton long before it became a mere gimmick. Jumbo once told me that his wife came of aristocratic Swedish origins. Their only child died in infancy, the sad event remembered by one of the stained-glass windows.

One of the flower ladies was a Miss Henbrey, who trimmed and arranged the blooms and ferny stuff by the church war memorial. Nearby was a window in memory of two second lieutenants killed in the Great War. Their young, boyish, smiling faces must have been typical of so many public school men with a brief training in the OTC (Officer Training Corps), which certainly never prepared them for the hideous nightmare of trench warfare. The window depicted them in medieval knight's armour. I think Miss Henbrey may have lost somebody dear in that conflict, which would explain her particular attention to the memorial. She was the Lady Superintendent at the Filstone Rest Home for Working Ladies in Belgrave Place, and I try to picture the residents. What were those working ladies resting from? And how did they now employ their time? Knitting, perhaps, crochet work or embroidery. Miss Henbrey was a prim spinster, but I think she had a soft spot for me. At the age of about five I used to tidy up the bits and pieces left over from her flower arranging and she would give me a few coppers reward. One Saturday she forgot and I asked for my 'wages'. She was amused and gave me the money, warning me not to tell my mother, for I

'I always remember my mother's hands: deeply etched and criss-crossed with the evidence of hard labour.'

had always been brought up to refuse tips for little jobs. Pride on my mother's part, I suppose. I think I was permitted three refusals, and then, if the tipper insisted, it was all right to accept.

Although Miss Henbrey was classified as an Old Girl by my mother, I think she should have married, because she liked children. She once came to a Sunday school treat at Burgess Hill and sat in a little shelter watching the children enjoy themselves. She beckoned me over and gave me half a crown, which was a munificent tip in the 30s. Mrs Baker was another flower lady, whose speciality was jumble sales and fetes. She used to make those expensive white lilies 'do twice' by trimming off the faded bits with nail scissors. I don't know whether they were jumble sale leftovers, but years later she gave me a set of Hume and Smollett's *History of England*, thirteen volumes in all, four volumes of Aikman's *History of Scotland*, a very early edition of Cruden's *Concordance*, which she had been using as a door stop, and three folio editions of Burnett's *History of Protestantism*. Generally speaking, then, the 'Old Girls Round the Church' were pleasant enough, with one exception as follows.

At the age of seven, I caught diphtheria and was taken away in a little van called the Tin Lizzy. When I asked my mother why she was crying, she pretended she was laughing. Diphtheria was of course a killer, mercifully almost unknown today in this country, and the first day I was at Bevendean Isolation Hospital a couple brought in a sick child, leaving shortly afterwards in tears. My stay there was miserable. The age range of the patients was wide, and at seven I must have been the youngest. I was bullied and teased. When I asked one of the older boys for a stamp and paper to write home he agreed provided I let him read the letter first. To the ward in general he read: 'Dear Mum, I hop you are well' which wasn't bad for a seven-year-old, but the object of much scornful mirth from the other patients. The nurses called you by your surname, the food was meagre, and you spoke to visitors once a week through a thick glass screen. One side of the ward overlooked a cemetery, a grim reminder of mortality, where my mother used to come on non-visiting days and wave to me. Your first week was flat on your back, and as you recovered, your head was raised, pillow by pillow until you were eventually allowed up. I remember an Oliver Twist incident when I joined another patient at a little table

Left side aisle with original 'free' pews. View of pulpit and Lady Chapel, behind which, through a little door in the panelling was my mother's cubby hole.

for tea. I snatched a piece of his cake and devoured it ravenously. The cry went up: 'Packham's stolen a cake.' No beadle and staff appeared, but my shame was abject. I did have one delicious meal there, and I told my mother afterwards it must have been a mistake and should have gone to a nurse. To return to the uncharitable Old Girl. When my mother mentioned that I had caught diphtheria her callous response was: 'Oh, dear! I hope he hasn't left any germs in the church.'

Behind the organ and through a little door under the pipes was my mother's cubby hole. There was a gas ring, brooms, brushes and other cleaning equipment plus a variety of vases and jars for the flowers, some smelling foul. It was a dark, dusty, musty sort of place where my mother used to brew up tea, fetching the water from a tap behind a curtain in the porch. My mother's cubby hole had been a vestry before the organ was installed, from which the choir processed at the beginning of the service. In a corner was the bell rope which Chatfield the Watchmaker pulled on Sundays, until the turret was removed after the Second World War for safety reasons. South westerly, salt-laden gales had eaten gaps in the stonework wide enough to put an arm through. The rope was threaded through a series of pulleys, leading eventually to the bell. Those pulleys needed oiling. The noisiest thing inside the church when Chatfield was pulling the rope was not the bell, but the squeal and rattle of the pulleys. Ringing that bell must have been a knack, because when Robert Stedman was installed as vicar in the 50s, he had to toll the bell to prove incumbency. All that could be heard was the rattling pulleys, sounding like a reluctant lavatory chain being tugged. He gave up in the end, so strictly speaking, I suppose the ceremony was incomplete. A case of somebody for whom the bell did not toll. Long after the turret was dismantled, the bell stood forlornly round the back of the church on a pile of rubble until one day two men came to collect it in a barrow. One of the churchwardens, Mr Ford, assumed the collection was official and gave the men a hand. He was not to know they were thieves hoping to make a pound or two from a scrap metal merchant.

The pews in the side aisles were free, labelled as such with a circular metal disc, recalling the influence of the two Wagners, who were anxious to provide seating for poorer parishioners. St Anne's was able to dispense with rented seats some five years before I was born, thanks to a rather mysterious gift mentioned in the minutes of the PCC (Parish Church Council) for October 1920. 'The Vicar informed the members of the Council that, whilst on holiday, he met a friend who gave him a sum of money which made it possible to make St Anne's an Entirely Free Parish and he was in hopes of it being an accomplished fact in a few months' time.' Who this generous friend was nobody will ever know, nor did the vicar mention the amount he gave. However, during the following October's meeting somebody asked whether there had been any complaints, now that the seats were all free. Apparently not. Were they expecting any, I wonder? No doubt people sat where they had always sat, and certainly my mother the church cleaner and I still sat on the 'free' side, under a window depicting the Nativity. I always liked this window, in warm sepia tones; with the shepherds and farm animals standing around the crib. Fortunately, it survived demolition when the East Window was smashed. I last saw it in an exhibition of church pictures and embellishments at the Brighton Art Gallery.

Later my mother and I shifted to a more central position near the pulpit, and we sat behind an Old Girl wearing what my mother described as a 'cake tin hat'. I called her the Mozzin Lady because in my childish imagination her head seemed to spin like a top emitting a soft humming sound. I suppose this poor woman had a nervous tremor which gave this effect. She was always smiling up at the vicar in the pulpit. The cake tin hat was secured by a pin, which fascinated me. I supposed that, as for earrings, the head had to be surgically pierced to allow the pin through. I wondered if her brain got damaged in the process.

My mother entertained me during the sermons by making handkerchief dolls. Well, a theological discourse would be well above the head of a five-year-old. The curate at this time was the Reverend Sidney Thomas, probably another Welshman, and I was alarmed by his pulpit manner. He seemed to be shouting at the congregation and making threatening gestures; but my mother assured me that he was in fact 'a very nice man'. There is but one criterion by which I judge a sermon. If the choirboys are listening, it's a good 'un. Sadly, this is seldom the case. I remember Canon James coming to a point in his sermon which ran something like this. 'And this is a precept which we could all follow' … then turning to the chancel … 'especially the choirboys, who are *talking*.' Then a long pause in which ears reddened and faces burned and Tozzer reached for his mark book. One visiting preacher occasioned much amusement at home. His theme must have been the Wonders of Creation and he returned again and again to 'the little leaf' which he somewhat unnecessarily informed us was beyond the wit of Man to make. His 'little leaf' became a catchword at home, always raising a laugh. Some preachers never appreciate the fact that simplicity is a most difficult art form whether pictorial or spoken. It isn't as easy as it looks. Alan Bennett's sermon with the text: 'Esau is an hairy man' should be mandatory study at all theological colleges. One preacher with charisma in full measure, pressed down and overflowing, was Dick Sheppard who used to hold open-air sermons up at the Devil's Dyke. The little steam train from Aldrington Halt was so overcrowded on one occasion that the engine gave up. I doubt whether I understood his sermons, but the man had a

Jumbo on the left, and curate, Reverend Sidney Thomas, right.
'He seemed to be shouting at the congregation and making threatening gestures; but my mother assured me that he was in fact a very nice man.'

magnetic personality and a wonderful sense of fun. He did not gain universal approval from Authority for throwing open the crypt of St Martin's in the Field to vagrants and prostitutes; but he deserves his final resting-place in the cloister green of Canterbury.

A few years later, when I was a pupil at St Mary's Junior Church School, Mount Street, a favourite teacher used to sit in front of us with her old mother. The service, alas, meant very little to me; but when she turned at the end and smiled, my Sunday was made. Then one day I committed some heinous crime at school – exactly what escapes my memory – and came up before my idol for verbal chastisement. 'If the people at St Anne's knew what a *wicked* boy you are, they wouldn't come to church', she assured me in ringing tones. I later pondered this in the light of the Ninety and Nine parable; but at the time I couldn't quite picture an empty church on my account. Miss Smithers, for that was the good lady's name, lived with her mother in Bloomsbury Place. A great privilege was to carry home her attache case, for which you were awarded tuppence a week. She was a frail, thin creature, given to fainting fits. I suppose she never had enough to eat; a teacher's pay those days was hardly princely. I remember her falling into the arms of Miss Mullins, an ancient crone who taught the reception class. Miss Smithers obviously had a mission for the Betterment of the Underprivileged Masses, because she once organised a children's film show in St Mary's Hall. Entrance fee was tuppence, and the subject of the first – and last – film was the *King George the Fifth* locomotive showing off its paces in America. The film was silent, of course, but an Old Girl in the audience carried on a commentary in a loud stage whisper. The following week I turned up with my tuppence to find a very large, antique magic lantern replacing the cinematograph. Slides were shown. At the end of the programme Miss Smithers asked us to indicate, by a show of hands, which we preferred: the cinematograph or the magic lantern. A forest of hands went up for the former and one or two – including mine because I was sorry for her – for the latter. 'They can't make up their minds' averred the Old Girl with the stage whisper. Tuppence was a formidable sum in those days, and anyway you could get into the Scratch (or King's Cliff Cinema) for thruppence.

Harvest Festivals before the last war were impressive

displays. Great mounds of produce were heaped against the choir stalls and round the chancel railings, which were decorated with sheaves of wheat. Apples, pears, grapes – all manner of fruit and vegetables spilled out over the marble floor and the fruity, bready smell filled the church. Sadly this abundance dwindled over the years until towards the end, the festival was little more than a token display. My mother used to squirrel away apples behind the big organ pipes over her cubby hole for my future consumption. Well, why not? Gleaning was an accepted practice in those days. The choir sang *Thou Visitest the Earth* by Maurice Greene; a lovely, joyful anthem with difficult little grace notes in the opening tenor passage. It was the first anthem I learned when I joined the choir in 1935.

The following year the church had to do without my mother for a month or two after she cracked her ribs falling on the iron scraper outside Stanmer Church. At the time I was on holiday at Littlehampton with Aunt Cissy and she didn't tell me. My summer holiday was cut short and my cousin Brenda took me home to our flat in Marine Terrace Mews. As soon as I entered the front door and smelt the embrocation I knew something was wrong. And there she was, sitting up in bed, her chest strapped with adhesive bandages. I was furious that I hadn't been told. Being fatherless, mother to me was my security: any threat to her life and limb threatened me. Canon James probably meant well when, on a visit he told her she was perhaps not *quite* ready to resume her work cleaning the church. Mother wasn't pleased. When she did return I helped with the Saturday morning cleaning, applying water to the coloured tiles with gusto. One Old Girl offered unasked advice. 'Don't you think you're using too much water?' Now I enjoyed a self-righteous glow when helping mother and expected praise rather than criticism. But I was generally a polite child so I mopped up the pool and held my tongue.

The verger was Mr Christian, who reminded me of one of those old retainers in a stately home, knowing his place but also knowing his worth, disappearing into the woodwork like a ghost - only Mr Christian disappeared into *The Burlington* across the way. When somebody once asked for the verger, the Vicar advised her to try 'the chemist's shop'.

The Patronal Festival Sunday, July 26th, was of course a special occasion and we processed round the church behind the banners of the various organisations. The hymn *Ye Pure in Heart* had been written for the coronation of Edward VII: a somewhat inappropriate title if applied to Teddy the Libertine. In the verse beginning: 'At last the march shall end' the procession stopped, to start again with renewed enthusiasm on the next verse. Well, what would it be today? Tambourines and synths? Twitching to electric guitars? On one of these ecumenical occasions when churches exchange visits I remember my hand being seized by a lady in what I imagined was an enthusiastic greeting. I was somewhat dismayed to learn that she wanted me to dance round the church with her. I suppose anything can look ridiculous according to your standpoint.

A dusty Union Jack drooped from a pole in the chancel, and I always understood this was because Earl Haig once visited St Anne's on Armistice Sunday. My mother said the church was jam-packed, with the temporary hinged pews being pressed into service. Canon James had won an MC at the Front, and he may have persuaded the Earl to attend his church. Old soldiers had a particular affection for Jimmy James, and he used to march at the head of the British Legion contingent down to the Brighton War Memorial, there to read the prayers. Well into his eighties the Canon continued this ritual until Archdeacon Booth tactfully suggested he should have a rest and let a younger man take over. At the church service we sang *O Valiant Hearts* and a bugler sounded *The Last Post*. Those days, the two minutes' silence was strictly observed, and I tried not to giggle when the maroon went off and we stood in silence behind our school desks. The ceremony continued until the Second World War, after which it gradually petered out until all but forgotten. In the early 1920's, however, a milkman nearly got mobbed when he continued working through the silence: the police had to escort him to safety.

Funerals were a bonus for the choirboys, and I think the going rate was one and thruppence a time. Two I remember in particular. Once we were ferried out to Ovingdean Church and were paid half a crown each. None of today's tinpot coins has the wonderfully solid feel of a half crown: real wealth to a boy of 1935. The other occasion was for Cicely Courtneidge's father: a very plush affair with showbiz personalities in attendance. My mother remembered one funeral with a shudder. All the way up the central aisle the coffin had leaked, and there were white drips which she had to mop up afterwards. What ailment the occupant of the coffin had died from I don't know; but my mother always said it was dropsy. Because of the drops, I suppose.

The Day Thou Gavest Lord is Ended will always remind me of balmy summer Sunday evenings with my mother waiting for me outside the vestry door while I changed out of cassock and surplice. We then took our customary promenade along Brighton front with me on the sharp lookout for discarded cigarette packets containing 'tab cards'. Wills used to issue a set which, when laid out in the right order formed a well-known picture. You then sent them away and received a copy for framing. Thus we acquired *Between Two Fires*, *The Laughing Cavalier* and we almost acquired one of *Mother and Son*, which depicted two horses in a field. I think the company made some numbered cards more difficult to get hold of, a ploy to make you smoke more cigarettes I suppose, and my mother thought they wouldn't notice if we sent in two of the same which seemed to fit. But they did notice, and we never received the picture and didn't get the cards back either.

We strolled through the holiday crowds, trippers with flat caps, open necked white shirts and white plimsolls and others, somewhat better dressed, from the Metropole and Grand. Once a middle aged man strolled by in the company of a little painted doll-like creature. I couldn't take my eyes off her, and my mother hurried me away. 'No wonder he looks ashamed of himself' she muttered, but never explained why. Those days boys learnt about sex from graffiti on lavatory walls or from half understood smutty remarks in the playground. Once I had an encounter on the beach with an unsavoury paedophile. I instinctively knew he was a bad 'un, particularly when he asked me to go to the pictures with him. I was late for choir practice and when Tozzer asked me why, I told him I had met a man on the beach and he had asked me to the pictures with him. You can imagine the ripple of laughter from the other choristers. Tozzer brought down his conducting cane with a thwack on the music desk and warned me to avoid such men in future. Of course, I mentioned the incident to my mother, who was horrified and distraught. 'I don't know what to do' she wailed, 'and you haven't got a father to explain things to you. You'd better ask your schoolmaster.' Ask him what? And of course, I didn't.

We crossed the Aquarium Terrace and reached the Aladdin's Cave by the Palace Pier. This was a subterranean funfair under the pavement itself, with slot machines, mirror maze and other attractions. 'Do here what you wouldn't do at home' invited the notice over the crockery smashing stall. You shied wooden balls at the plates on the shelves, a good way, presumably of getting rid of pent-up frustration. The proprietor of the stall was quite canny: he delayed replacing the crockery until the last fragment had been smashed. Where did he buy the replacements, I wonder? I was most fascinated by the piano and violin machine. Instead of a bow, little rollers pressed over the strings while hammers struck away lustily behind. It was an ingenious piece of mechanism, certainly worth a penny a go. The last I saw of it was during the last war when rolls of barbed wire kept the public and, supposedly, the Germans off the front. The Aladdin's Cave was then in a sorry state of dilapidation with wistful reminders of happier, pre-war days. My favourite violin and piano machine had been wrecked.

Sunday evening was rounded off with an ice cream from Gizzi's Ice Cream Parlour at the bottom of St James' Street;

and mother and I sat between the two Russian cannon in Old Steine Gardens. They were broken up during the war and melted down. While I finished off my ice cream my mother watched the world go by peacefully – a rare luxury for a woman always on the go – and then home.

The clearest picture in my mind of those far off days will always be of my mother, armed with her mop and bucket and always wearing a smile, doing her Saturday morning cleaning. She no doubt found time, like Mr Christian the verger, to slip away to the chemist's shop for her customary Guinness. Saturdays were corned beef and Smith's Crisp lunches because she had little time to prepare anything more elaborate. Sometimes this would be followed by a slice of Zulu Cake from Giggins, a most delicious confection with a chocolate layer on top, spongy interior, and a thick layer of real cream.

Picture opposite: Choir stalls, altar with carving of Last Supper, and reredos.

Quires and Places Where They Sing

When I mentioned that I was about to join a choir, Mr Cooper the assistant head of St Mary's, who was not given to compliments, conceded that I had a good voice. Well, so I had. Mind you, joining St Anne's choir in 1935 was no pushover. Today even cathedral schools seldom suffer an embarrassment of suitable probationers; and parish churches usually have more women than boys, so the selection process at St Anne's would seem stringent by comparison. Beyond all doubt, our choir, we were convinced, was second to none, and that included the Parish Church of St Peter. We were put to the test in 1936 when we entered a competition at the Dome against the parish churches of Brighton and Hove. There were only the three, and we came third; the adjudicator unkindly remarking that our singing lacked beauty. Mr Hatchard the assistant choirmaster said ruefully that this was just about the most damning criticism you could fling at a choir. Music without beauty just isn't music. Choirboys were very jealous of their reputation in those days, and once I was nearly martyred for it. I happened to mention to a chorister of St Mary's, to which my school was attached, that St Anne's was tops. His minder was Fadden, a bully boy prefect who was also a chorister of St Mary's. He stopped me at the school gate and challenged my claim. Poltroonly I backed down, with metaphorical fingers crossed behind my back.

As the voices of the older boys broke, the Vicar made his appeal for probationers from the pulpit and in the parish magazine. Membership of the choir would be a privilege, he said and a chance to learn music. For the first few weeks the new boys attended the three practices a week, which included a full one with the men on Fridays. But they didn't sing with the choir on Sundays: this was the next stage when they sat at the back in cassock and surplice, entering and leaving unobtrusively by a side door. By this time you were pretty familiar with the order of the service and had learnt one or two of the set canticles and anthems. While still a probationer and sitting with my mother in the church I couldn't resist joining in the harvest anthem. The first Magnificat I learnt was Stanford in BFlat which remains my favourite. Then finally came the Sunday when you processed out from the vestry behind Chatfield the Crucifer, followed by the choir gentlemen. But the awesomeness soon wore off, and you began drawing cartoons on the backs of the hymn sheets during the sermon with the best of them. The subjects were usually the choirmen with rude comments, providing amusement for my mother when she found them while dusting the choir stalls.

On Good Friday we processed in with great solemnity minus surplices to sing Stainer's *Crucifixion*. 'Fling Wide the Gates' has some risky, overlapping phrases which can often degenerate into chaos, and the relief was palpable if we got through it without mishap. 'God So Loved The World', probably the finest thing Stainer ever wrote we sang unaccompanied, more often than not dropping a semitone by the end. Then came that powerful chorus 'From The Throne of His Cross' in which we boys were forbidden to smile. Usually Tozzer told us to look as though we enjoyed singing, but once when practising this particular chorus he blew his top when he saw a boy grinning. Anscombe, who probably had the most unlovely voice I have ever heard, always got a robber's part to sing. Type casting I suppose, for his was a brutish, gravelly voice. Stainer is regarded as sugary and sentimental today, but given a good choir in top form with professional soloists, the *Crucifixion* can still move, deeply. I believe the poor man endured frequent requests from vicars to write music for their verses and this would explain much. Perhaps his music is dated; but we'll have to wait a long time to judge whether many modern composers will find themselves rubbing shoulders with Bach and Handel. I doubt many will enjoy that privilege.

Easter day was a brilliant occasion with the fragrance of spring flowers and the choir in freshly laundered surplices that almost cracked with the starching. There must have been some overcast Easter Sundays but I honestly cannot remember one. Glorious sunshine flooded the church, setting off to advantage the new hats and Easter dresses of the ladies in the congregation and glinting on the brasswork. We processed round the church singing *Jesus Christ Is Risen Today* with all those lengthy, joyful alleluias, catching the eyes of mums and dads as we passed and getting a smile in response. Every niche was decorated with blossom and greenery, and thanks to my mother and the Old Girls with their tins of Bluebell and chamois leathers, the church was sparkle clean.

But of course we boys enjoyed the Christmas music best of all. The carols had been rehearsed for several weeks, and readers chosen for the nine lessons. A young choirboy was usually picked to read one of these and I was thankful for being spared an ordeal in which I would surely have dried up. Years later I read lessons quite often, and once at very short notice. We were processing up the central aisle when Jumbo prodded me in the ribs. 'Could you read the second lesson?' The regular hadn't turned up. There are of course pitfalls in lesson reading. Once I turned over two pages, ploughing on until I came to a likely stop, but of course the second page was a complete non sequitur, leaving the congregation bewildered. I apologised to Jumbo afterwards, but he smiled kindly and said: 'It's not the first time and it won't be the last.' Punctuation is absolutely vital in one of the Christmas readings. '….and found Mary and Joseph, and the babe lying in a manger.' A tight squeeze if you forget the comma. Then there was the time when a reader was given Matthew One by mistake with that long genealogical passage, and all those Biblical names.

The carol service always started off in the vestry with *Hark What Mean Those Holy Voices?* and as we couldn't see the organist nor hear the instrument very clearly in that boxed-in atmosphere we raced ahead, ending up a bar or two in front. Then, as we began to process round the church a boy sang the first verse of *Once In Royal David's City*.

On Christmas Eve the boys sang carols at the Workhouse at the top of Elm Grove, then as now, a gaunt, forbidding pile renamed The General Hospital. White-haired, frail old women dressed in blue uniforms sat round a deal table that had been scrubbed so vigorously over the past seventy odd years that deep channels had been scored in the surface. *In The Bleak Mid Winter* was certainly appropriate to the occasion and place. At the end of the carols Tozzer pointed to Peter Symonds, a diminutive chorister and said: 'This is the Tom Thumb of our company.' Starved of family affection for heaven knows how many years the poor old things pressed the embarrassed boy to their withered bosoms.

Walking home on a brisk winter's evening down Freshfield Road with Tozzer Witcombe we looked forward to the following Christmas Day morning with the presents and the festive food to follow.

In the 20s, when my brother George was a choirboy, the Christmas treat included tea at the creamery in Pavilion Buildings. Ten years later we didn't get the tea but were taken to the pantomime at the end of the Palace Pier. In those days they were traditional, sticking pretty closely to the story line, and very great fun. The dames were delightfully vulgar but nice, and somehow respectable. Unlike today, the show wasn't padded out with speciality acts irrelevant to the plot, nor were they vehicles for soap actors or plugs for sporting personalities whose histrionic talent is nil. There was no sleaze. Just before the grand scene at the end when all the cast came down the staircase, a screen came down in front of the main curtain with the latest comic ditty. Buttons, or whoever was the funny man of the show, encouraged the audience to sing, dividing us up to compete against each other. Once Canon James went backstage during the interval and had a word with the comic. When it came to our turn to sing he said: 'I can tell that's St Anne's choirboys in the balcony: their voices aren't as beery as the rest of you.' When it came to publicity, Jumbo never missed a trick.

He had another chance to advertise the choir just before Christmas 1936. 'The *Brighton and Hove Herald* wanted a photograph of the best choir in Brighton so naturally they came to St Anne's,' he said. The photographer arrived on the Friday, which was full practice night and we all changed into cassocks and surplices. The first photo was taken on the Cantoris side with Tozzer at the organ peeping impishly round the corner. We were all holding copies of Somervell's *Christmas* but it didn't look right somehow. Well, of course it didn't because we weren't actually singing. So we all moved over to the Decani side and Tozzer made us sing 'loo' before the flash, and as we all had our mouths open it looked quite convincing. The picture appeared in the *Brighton and Hove Herald* decorated with a border of holly and looked very festive.

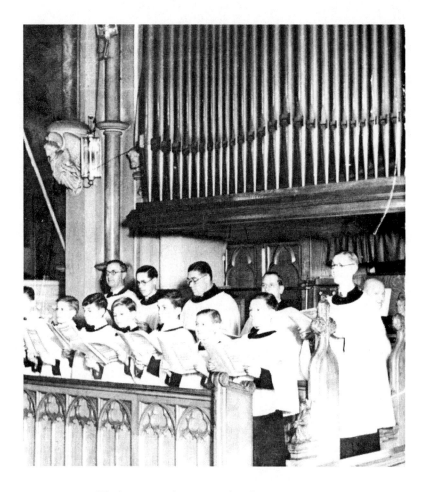

Christmas photograph, first attempt. Mouths firmly closed and Tozzer peeping impishly round the corner. Maurice in the front row, fourth from right. Assistant choirmaster, Mr Hatchard, bespectacled, second row, first right.

Jumbo was proud of his choir and sang a good tenor which didn't disgrace his Welsh origins. But if I'm strictly honest I must admit that some of the men's voices were far below concert standard. I'd always describe myself as a 'bread and butter' baritone with a fair ability to read a line of music at sight, but certainly never solo material. In the 30s we had a tenor who 'scooped', that is, he had a nasty habit of sliding from one note to another. When Tozzer Witcombe once ticked off a boy for doing just this, I suggested the culprit had caught the habit from one of the choirmen. Tozzer was honest enough not to comment or deny. Langley had an excellent bass voice; and Sidney Beckett was a good tenor but with an inclination to overdo the tremolo. He used to sing in the church concerts and his favourite was *Marta Rambling Rose of the Wildwood* accompanying himself on the piano accordion. Chatfield the Watchmaker was an alto, a species of voice I had never before encountered when I joined the choir as a boy, and I found it strange to hear a man singing falsetto. He had a strong voice, was always on pitch, but his enunciation was poor. Lelliot the Builder sang a passable tenor as did Rogers the Scooper. Another tenor was Saunders, an ornamental ironworker whom I nicknamed Gorilla Face though he was a kindly man. He was another scooper and his party piece was *Seek Ye The Lord*; and I can still hear him singing the opening passages, sliding up and down as he went. There was a very old man with a white walrus moustache. This was Mr Viney, a carpenter by trade, who had premises in Sloane Street Brighton. His daughter was a music teacher. I don't know what part he sang, but he

Christmas photograph, second attempt.
Mouths open wide, singing to 'loo'. Tozzer
extreme right, Jumbo in front of pillar and
top boy Phillip Jarman to his right.
Choirman with shining spectacles is
Chatfield the Watchmaker.

never missed a practice or service. Mr Handley was another
alto whom I've mentioned elsewhere as one of the trio who
sang comic songs at church concerts. With all their short-
comings and unmusical habits, the choirmen of St Anne's
produced a good, honest sound, thanks in good measure to
the skill of the choirmaster, Tozzer.

I wonder if any church choir today enjoys the fellowship
felt by us in the 30s. There was, of course, a rigidly observed
hierarchy among the boys when probationers were much

below the salt. Top boys were regarded with something short of reverence, which is surprising if you bear in mind that there couldn't have been a big age gap between them and the youngsters. If a glance from the top boy did not quell, then the bony finger of a choirman poked the culprit in the back; and if this failed Tozzer might catch his eye in the organ mirror, frown and reach for the mark book. A carpeting from the vicar was rare, and to my recollection only happened once. Some of the boys had joined the Boy Scouts and as there wasn't a St Anne's troop, choir practice and scout night clashed. Of course the answer would have been to form a scout troop at St Anne's, as envisaged when the church hall was opened in 1912; but Jumbo simply told the boys to make up their minds which they belonged to, scouts or choir, as they couldn't belong to both.

Present day cathedral choristers have a pretty rigorous routine but of course they are a special and rare breed. But I don't think boys today would put up with the demands of St Anne's in the 30s. We had three practices a week, and on the first Sunday in the month, those of us who had been confirmed would already have attended eight o'clock communion, followed by a Sung Eucharist at nine thirty, Matins at eleven, Children's Service in the afternoon, the Evening Service, followed by a rather pointless service called The Guild Of The Holy Family in which Jumbo would give a desultory little chat.

The Organ

Let the pealing organ blow,
To the full-voiced quire below.
                                Milton

Jumbo always included the organ blower in his list of thanks at PCC (Parochial Church Council) meetings. Who this gentleman was we shall never know; but his labours ceased when the instrument was electrified, and he disappears from the minute book.

Organ blowers must always be taken seriously as one of Tozzer's anecdotes demonstrates. One such always insisted on – and was never denied – a copy of the music to be played. A visiting organist of haughty mien turned down the old man's request. 'Why on earth do you need a copy?' he demanded; and the aggrieved blower shuffled off to his pumping lever behind the organ. Well of course you can guess what happened. The organist flexed his fingers for a virtuoso performance of Handel's *Hallelujah Chorus* and was then rewarded with subterranean gurgling sounds. Incensed, he took the blower to task afterwards. 'How was I to know it was the *Hallelujah Chorus*?', muttered the aggrieved pumper.

The Henry Willis, installed in the 1870s, must have been a very welcome improvement on the harmonium played by the Vicar's wife. A Willis organ is the Rolls Royce of the species; and thanks to his energy and long working life there are many surviving, producing that richness and delicacy of tone for which he was so justly famed. Sadly, some have been allowed to deteriorate, others have been 'mucked about with' by less skilful hands, and others broken up. Henry Willis would of course have seen the application of electricity before his death in 1901, and added many improvements of his own. With Wesley he introduced radiating, concave pedals, he improved pneumatic action, and invented pedal and manual couplers which he used in all his instruments for over sixty years. But his most valuable contribution must be the Full

Swell Organ. All these were features of the organ at St Anne's Church.

Organs are – organic. They grow through the years with additional stops and other refinements. Some cathedral instruments have pipes going back to the seventeenth century – and even earlier – with additions made only yesterday. When Morgan and Smith rebuilt St Anne's organ in 1922 it was decided to add the Open Diapason and Tromba when funds were available. In the event, with a little creative accountancy and postponing the appointment of a curate, these stops were in fact included when the organ was rebuilt.

The Vicar laid before the meeting the great advantage of having two extra stops added to the organ: an Open Diapason stop and a Tromba. These would give an extra finish to the organ. To have the Open Diapason added, the Vicar was willing to forgo having a curate until after June and to use the money allocated from the Free Will Offering fund, viz:- £70 and £10 from the Free Concerts would pay the cost.…. It was suggested by the Vicar if the Builders would be willing to wait for a time for their money, which he no doubt thought they would do, it would better to complete the organ and be more satisfactory to them. These three (?) extra stops mentioned in the specification could be added at any time.…

I trust when the Reverend Sidney Thomas, the new curate heard the open diapason, he realised his true worth.

For many years the organ at St Anne's had been allowed to fall into disrepair and was frequently mentioned in the PCC minutes. In the second meeting in June 1920, for instance, is the following:

It was unanimously carried that a Bazaar should be held to help raise Funds for the restoration of the organ.

The redoubtable Miss Waldron headed the Ladies' Committee. How much they raised we don't know, but seemingly not much because a year later:

The Vicar spoke on the Organ Fund and stated that the organ was in a deplorable condition at the present time.

At a future meeting the Vicar read a lengthy report and specification from Morgan and Smith about the condition of the organ. Their estimate for rebuilding was £1200, which must have dismayed the PCC because by June 1921 they had raised only £412. Amazingly, by December of that same year the fund had shot up to £1124. By what manner or means, or from what charitable donor, we shall never know; but they were now in a position to ask for tenders.

Messrs Willis' price was £2000, Hills' £2060 while Morgan and Smith of Hove asked £1450. Before going any further the Vicar asked the advice of Mr Stanley Roper, organist of HM Chapel Royal, St James' Palace; and this very eminent musician said that he'd like to inspect some of Morgan and Smith's work before making up his mind. This rather suggests that the cheapest tender, Morgan and Smith's had already been decided on, or could it be that Mr Stanley Roper had no doubts about the excellence of the other two organ builders and did not think inspection of their work necessary? However, on Saturday, June 24th 1922 he inspected the instrument at St Bartholomew's Church together with others in Brighton and wrote to say that he was thoroughly satisfied with what he had seen and 'had no hesitation in recommending the acceptance of this firm's tender'. He was paid thirty guineas for his advice and given the responsibility of supervising Morgan and Smith's work.

After completion, a contract was taken out with Morgan and Smith making them responsible for defects or breakages 'apart from those caused by water, damp or wilful misuse'. How do you 'wilfully misuse' an organ I wonder? Play Heavy Metal on it, I suppose.

Jumbo was always touchy about the organ. In his latter years criticism was voiced about the choir box and swell. The only way of increasing the volume on a wind organ is by means of opening a Venetian shutter device in front of the pipes. This is operated by a foot pedal, and as the moving parts are quite heavy there is an ingenious system of counterbalancing weights. Clearly you can't increase the volume by blowing harder because the wind pressure has to be precisely right to make any sound at all. For the best effects of course, the shutter device should be as near the front as possible; but for some reason known only to himself, Stanley Roper put the choir box in front of the swell, thus reducing its effect. When a latter day Willis visited St Anne's in the 1950s his remarks about this arrangement were unsuitable for the interior of a church. However, Jumbo quoted the opinion of a local broadcasting organist, Douglas Reeve, who assured him that it was a very fine instrument.

As a choirboy sitting on the Decani side I was always fascinated to see the huge bellow behind the pipes slowly inflating. It never crossed my mind at the time to consider what an ingenious piece of mechanism this really was. The top was weighted so as to express the air, and the sides concertina'd like a piano accordion. Of course it is essential that the pressure of the air remains constant, and it is not immediately apparent that this tends to increase as the bellows close: the other way round seems more likely. The reason is that the smaller the pocket of air inside the bellows, the less the weight on top is cushioned. To compensate for this, Alexander Cummings invented bellows with 'inverted folds' so that the pressure remains the same throughout the rise and fall.

I was always puzzled by a sweet sandalwoody smell emerging from the organ from time to time. When the organ was dismantled after the closure of St Anne's I was able to look at it from the inside. Then I understood; for some of the pipes were stepped in mahogany – hence the sweet smell. Much of the organ was rescued; some of it is now in store, and the Tromba, which caused so much heart searching in the 1920s is now in the church of St Mary de Haura at Shoreham

G. H. Witcombe
(1873 – 1966)

Or as he was affectionately nicknamed Tozzer, organist and choirmaster at St Anne's deserves a special mention of his own. My brother, ten years my senior, rather unfairly described him as a Mr Pecksniff; but in his best mood he was a jolly, rotund little man who bounced cheerfully down Burlington Street to unlock the vestry door for choir practice. He continued to bounce well into his eighties, taking a cold bath every morning. I don't think he was ever ill. My brother also conceded that he was a very fine musician, and nobody who heard him perform on the organ would disagree with this opinion.

His academic background was not impressive, and early examination results do not reflect any musical leanings, nor his later fine abilities. He went to school at Sanford Street, Swindon where at sixteen he was made pupil teacher. This was hardly an enviable position, rather akin to a Royal Naval midshipman: neither fully accepted by the wardroom nor entirely feared by the lower deck; but he was promoted to assistant master some years later. His musical career seems to have begun at King Edward's School, Witley in Surrey where he was assistant master and organist for a year. He gained his teaching qualifications at St Gaul's College, Cheltenham obtaining a Board of Education Certificate in Chemistry, Agriculture, Physiography – whatever that may be – and Physiology. This last proved invaluable in later years when he developed his own very successful treatment for asthmatics. A friend of mine who went into the RAF told me that but for Tozzer's treatment, he would never have passed the medical. His special subjects were Music and History.

His Brighton teaching career began at the old York Place School, which did not enjoy the status of a Grammar, but the syllabus included subjects not usually taught at elementary schools. There is a photograph of Tozzer in the school magazine, standing with folded arms among the members of the school orchestra, almost all of them wearing the mandatory Eton collar and knickerbockers. This must have been about 1904 when E B Lethbridge was headmaster. An account of a school concert appears in the *Sussex Daily News*:

> *Pupils' entertainments as a rule are 'terrible things' but the entertainment given at the Dome on Thursday by the pupils of York Place Higher Grade School was entirely different ... The programme was opened with an organ solo by Mr G H Witcombe who gave a brilliant interpretation of Rudyard Kipling's 'Absent Minded Beggar' and won well deserved applause.*

In the early years of this century Tozzer was frequently called upon to play the organ at the Dome for charity concerts and school treats. His first appointment as a church organist was at St Mark's, Kemp Town.

There are frequent references in the PCC minutes to the parlous state of the organ at St Anne's. In the January meeting for 1921 the vicar stated 'that the organ was in a deplorable condition' and thereafter bazaars and other fundraising events were organised with renovation in view. There were not only problems with the instrument. In May 1923 Mr Saffets the organist resigned with no reason given in the minutes and the vacancy was advertised. This was filled by Mr A W Fisher, who resigned on the grounds of ill health only a year later. The appointment of a new organist was left in abeyance, and the next candidate, Mr Pym Browning couldn't find a house. The assistant organist Mr Wright filled in until a permanent one could be found. Mr Pym Browning then makes a re-entrance, having presumably found a house. He started in June 1925 at a salary of £80 with an extra payment – probably a one-off – for his removal expenses, of £10. Alas, Mr Pym Browning didn't find his house after all and resigned in September, leaving an opening for Tozzer Witcombe, who held the post until 1946.

Tozzer was a perfectionist, demanding high standards from both men and boys and possessed some of the talent of Malcolm Sargent in getting a good sound from less than professional singers. Like other choirmasters he had strange notions about voice production. He told us boys to imagine a hole in the middle of our foreheads through which the voice emerged and insisted we hold the music with both hands – not just forefinger and thumb – but I suspect his main concern was for the wear and tear of the sheet music.

He devised his own, and probably unique system of paying choirboys. Probationers were paid a penny a service, rising by halfpennies to about tuppence halfpenny for top boys. Soloists were paid extra – thruppence I think – and there were extra payments for marriages and funerals. He kept his records in a black book on a shelf near the organ, and made a great show of opening it, glowering over his spectacles and giving a 'black mark' to any offender. Double marks were awarded for meritorious service. On quarter day he would tell us that the choir's pay came from his own bank, not from a church account, to make us feel suitably grateful, I suppose. 'We can't pay you what you're really worth' he'd say to give us a warm glow, 'this is just pocket money.' But this sentiment was contradicted during the payout.

There he'd sit, behind the baize table in the vestry with neat little piles of coins and his mark book open. You waited for your name to be called and then stepped forward. A pile of coins was pushed across the green baize. But just as your hand was about to enclose it – 'Packham! Are you *worth* it?' This put you in a dilemma. To say 'yes' sounded like cheek, but if you said 'no' the money might be clawed back. The best plan was to say nothing but look suitably contrite. For some peccadillo during choir practice he would sometimes bring down his conducting cane with a thwack on the music desk and tick the boy off. He'd then tell the miscreant how much his crime would cost. On one occasion I unintentionally passed wind and Tozzer replied 'That, Packham will cost you half a crown!' Tears of helpless laughter ran down my cheek at the notion that a fart was so expensive. A case of inflation, I suppose. Tozzer made me stand by the War Memorial 'until my thoughts were cleaner'.

When a chorister went too far, Tozzer would shout in feigned fury, 'Get out!' the boy would make his way in silence and shame to the vestry door. He never got there because Tozzer would call out, just in time, 'Stop! What are you here for, to fool about or work?' The boy usually gave the right answer. 'Come back and work then' said Tozzer. But one of the cheekier boys, Tuppenny White, when asked to return and work, put a finger coyly under his chin and said 'no'. Then left. He'd called Tozzer's bluff.

Tozzer had a kindly streak in his nature. There was an old character trudging about Kemp Town called Mr McKay. He had seen better times and may once have been an actor, for despite his shabby appearance he had a noble face and a distinguished nose. He may very well have been the park story teller that my mother remembered, holding a cluster of childen spellbound with tales. He loved to sit at the back of the choir stalls when we were practising, and when the boys had left Tozzer accompanied him on the organ. 'He hasn't much of a voice' said Tozzer, 'but he likes to sing.' Tozzer persuaded him to give a dramatic recital after choir practice one day. Mr McKay chose Clarence's dream from *Richard III*. If I'd heard of Henry Irving at the time I should have noted a resemblance. The performance was good, highly emotional. Tozzer showed his kindly streak on another occasion when I was looking wistfully at some strawberry tarts in a baker's window. He happened by, and gave me tuppence to buy one.

I think there must have been a rift developing between Tozzer and Jumbo. Certainly Tozzer had the energy and ability to go on for a few years more – probably several, and I shall never know the cause of his leaving. He told me he had 'mixed feelings' about it. Both men, James and Witcombe were strong personalities; and I can remember the Canon suggesting that we took a piece of music we were practising at a different speed. Whether slower or faster, I can't remember; but 'that's the tempo they take it at Chichester Cathedral' said Jumbo. 'We'll take it at this tempo here' was Tozzer's rather brusque rejoinder.

An obituary in the *Dolphin*, the magazine of Varndean Grammar School, remembers Tozzer's long teaching career and his devoted service to Varndean in its middle years. Special tribute was paid to his success in dealing with speech defects and his treatment of breathing problems. 'He was one of a small but unfortuntely diminishing band of devoted men who gave so much for so long to the development of Varndean ... and as a nonagerian was a very welcome guest at the Old Varndeanian annual dinners. Varndean will always honour him as one of the makers of the school.'

Mayor and five Masters: (left to right) R S Newsam; P Trustram;The Mayor; A Lea Perkins; A C Atkinson; G H Witcombe. Courtesy of the Argus

Sunday School Treats

The summer treat for the infant classes was held in the Hall, the children seated each side of long trestle tables. The little cakes were always the same sort: diamond-shaped with pink and white icing. 'Don't start on the cakes until you've finished up the bread and butter and paste sandwiches.' Tea was of the urn variety, which as anybody who has ever tasted it remembers, had a distinct but indescribable flavour: possibly somewhat metallic, certainly weak and anaemic. Vicars are probably warned of this brew at theological colleges and trained to imbibe it without a shudder. After tea in the Hall the children were crocodiled up to Manor Farm, now submerged beneath a housing estate. Here they had games.

Once there was a violent thunderstorm and we were all hustled into a corrugated iron hut: not a really good idea because one unlucky strike and a future St.Anne's congregation would have been incinerated. One terrified little boy by the name of Eastwood sobbed uncontrollably. 'He's spoilt!' declared one unsympathetic Old Girl. When the rain cleared, the remaining cakes from the tea party were brought up to the manor field in a basket, and we were formed into a moving circle, dipping into the baskets as we passed.

The seniors went by train to Hassocks and enjoyed a day at the pleasure gardens there. A most attractive feature was the lake with little boats driven by hand-turned paddle wheels. An excursion train was laid on from the old Kemp Town Station, now an industrial site, where we assembled with our packed lunches, excited at the prospect of going through a murky tunnel under Freshfield Road and Elm Grove, and so across the viaduct over Lewes Road. The station had been closed for ordinary passenger traffic since 1932, so you could say our trip was something special. Hassocks pleasure garden must have closed, because the following year we went instead to the Victoria Gardens at Burgess Hill, now under bricks and mortar. We went in a coach of somewhat ancient vintage, open to the weather with a fold-back cover, and the long seat at the back was entirely occupied by one family: the Cattaways. My mother came too.

There was another lake at the Victoria Gardens with canoes and rowing boats. When your money ran out there were free swings and slides; and a very adequate space in which to run wild. The noisiest feature was a roundabout, which endlessly played the hit song for 1928, *If I Had A Talking Picture of You.* It used to go crazy, blaring out a devilish roar devoid of melody or harmony. To this day I am not sure whether this was a mechanical fault or intentional. Whatever, it was a dreadful sound. The penny-catching side stalls were run by a family which took over for the season, a singularly humourless lot with none of your 'Roll Up, Roll Up!' enthusiasm of the Palace Pier funfair. I never saw anybody win a prize on the Tumbling Tanks. These were metal, rhomboidal boxes with a heavy weight inside which made them tip over and roll down a slope. If yours fell in a hole and rang a bell you got a prize. Some hopes! Occasionally the man running the stall would push one of the tanks down a hole, ringing the bell to show how easy it was. Then there was Roll the Penny, with squares showing the amount you won if your penny stopped exactly inside the square without touching the sides. Even without the aid of the modern computer somebody must have worked out the near impossibility of this happening, and native instinct warned me to risk few pennies on this venture. My favourite was the Trolleys which cost a ha'penny. These were rather beautifully made of polished wood: little chairs affixed to a base with wheels. Compared to what's on offer today at any funfair: virtual reality; gut-twisting rides; horrific devices to fling you into the air, turn you upside down, turn you round and over, all within an inch of instant death, the Trolleys would seem very tame. But, of course, we knew no better. At the end of the ride down the narrow track we were expected to bring the trolley back. However, we used to push it half-way up and snatch another free ride, with the man at the top waving his arms about and shouting at us. Bicycle rides were a penny a time; and there was a variety of machines to choose from.

Tea was held in a huge iron shed rather like an oversized Nissen hut. The time honoured urn tea was provided together with sandwiches and cakes. During the tea, churchwardens came round and placed a sixpence on each plate. We considered very carefully how this largess should be expended.

One summer, another terrific rainstorm confined us to the iron shed, the downpour thundering on the roof. Volunteers were invited to sing, dance and otherwise entertain. I don't know who it was, but a child from my school, St Mary's Junior Mixed, suggested that Kathleen Whiteman and Maurice Packham could say a poem together. 'Oh no they can't', thought I, panic stricken at the very notion. We had learnt Harold Munro's *Overheard in a Salt Marsh*, which is a duologue between some species of deformed troll and a fairy. He begs a necklace from her and she resolutely refuses to part with it. The troll becomes more and more impassioned but to each appeal Kathleen Whiteman had merely to answer 'No!' Hers was not a seductive, teasing refusal. She was snappish, like a mother refusing a penny to an importunate child. In front of my favourite teacher, Miss Dawson, I quite enjoyed showing off my histrionic skill. Anyway, I had the best lines. But unable to face the assembled company in the iron hut I fled into the storm, heedless of the drenching downpour.

Sadly, the Victoria Pleasure Gardens are no more and the entertainments there on offer belong to a vanished, more innocent world. But once it was a favourite choice for Sunday School treats, and long before we visited the place in the 30s there had been a steam paddleboat on the lake, and a switchback, which actually crossed the water. The iron hut where we had our tea could seat 1,500 and a 1900 leaflet describes what was on the menu: 'High-class refreshments, dairy produce, hot and cold luncheons and afternoon teas.' Mr Edwin Street opened the gardens in celebration of Queen Victoria's Diamond Jubilee; and special excursion trains used to run from Brighton and Eastbourne. A note on the leaflet warns, 'These gardens are opened on strictly temperance principles.' Lager-louts evidently not welcomed. The gardens were closed in 1939 and were left neglected until built over in 1954.

The Church Hall

A glittering occasion took place in Brighton's fashionable month of October in 1912, when the winkle and whelk hordes had long since returned to London and the *haut ton* had taken up autumn residence in Lewes Crescent, Sussex Square and Marine Parade. Everybody of any consequence in Kemp Town came to see the Bishop of Chichester declare the new St Anne's Hall officially opened.

Gaitered and aproned he sat on the platform in solemn splendour amongst the potted ferns and floral decorations in the company of the Mayor and Mayoress, Alderman and Mrs Thomas-Stanford, Eliza Nixon the 'generous donor of the institute' – and Mr Evershed the Grocer.

So there they all sat facing a hall packed with a large gathering of parishioners and friends.

Ever since his appointment in 1909 the Vicar, T J James had regretted the lack of a church hall. 'We held our Sunday School in the church' he said. 'Everything had to be held in the church, but we drew the line at Mothers' Meetings and Sewing Parties.'

Occasionally they had been granted accommodation at St Mary's, just up the road; but they had no home of their own. Only a few months before the official opening, a church hall seemed a remote dream, with mere promises of money. Then Mrs Nixon, a wealthy parishioner stepped in. 'I am going to build an institute for you' she said, and the church hall became a reality. The gift was in memory of her husband John Nixon, JP, who was the first pioneer of the South Wales Steam Coal trade.

The proceedings were opened when little Joyce Bright in her best frock and with her nicest curtsey presented Mrs Nixon with a bouquet of flowers. Then the Bishop launched forth about the recreative needs of Man. 'If you are going to reach the souls of the people you must care for their bodies, their minds and their recreations. Rightly used the church institute will do a work that the parson and the church can never do by themselves.' Always a good whipping boy those days, Demon Drink got a mention. 'You may preach temperance or teetotalism till you are blue in the face; but unless you provide some recreative place it is no good telling men that they must not go to the public house, which to them is their club.' One can hear his ringing tones and see the responsive nods in the audience; but within spitting distance were four pubs, the nearest being the *Northumberland Arms* on the opposite corner of Crescent Place. Just across the road was the *Burlington*, the frequent resort of Mr Christian the Verger and which the Vicar euphemistically termed 'the chemist's shop'. The Mayor then congratulated the parish on the acquisition of such a fine hall and the speeches were rounded off by the Reverend T J James proposing a vote of thanks to Mrs Nixon.

But the Bishop had the last word. He said the furnishing of the institute had cost about £300 leaving a shortfall of £260. 'Why don't we all pay for our chair?' He waved a note in the air. 'As a lead, I will give five pounds.' That must have taken the smile off a few faces.

In 1912 the church hall would have been considered state of the art. There was even a projection room above the gallery: 'a fireproof chamber for a cinematographic lantern'. At the back of the stage were the Gentlemen's and Ladies' Retirement Rooms for the actors. There was a proscenium of sorts, painted canvas on a wooden frame. The red plush curtain rolled up on a long pole operated by a rope on the prompt side. I can remember only one scene-drop: a rural scene with a cottage. Stage right was a Tudorish window flat; and wings could be slid into wooden forks above the stage. A stone staircase descended to a cellar under the stage, which a later generation called the Devil's Kitchen, described at the official opening as 'a large drill hall for the Boy Scouts'. It was later used as a club room for the older boys of the parish, and there was a full-sized billiard table and a bookcase containing, as I remember, a few Victorian volumes. A gas ring and sink provided facilities for brewing up tea and coffee.

Frankly, it was a cheerless place, lit by ground level frosted windows giving on to Crescent Place, and the atmosphere was hardly improved by the chocolate brown paint, which covered all the walls. Of course the architects, Denman Matthews had been presented with something of a problem. A cramped site had been found on the corner of St George's Road and Crescent Place; and one side of the hall was blind. The main lighting came through a large skylight, above which was a very big cowl, swivelling in the wind, very necessary for the ventilation of a hall heated by gas radiators. I doubt whether this system would have met official approval today and it is surprising that on cold winter's days audiences weren't gassed by carbon monoxide. Within the limits of such a narrow compass, then, the architects had, as the *Brighton Herald* stated 'united efficiency with economy to a remarkable degree'.

In my childhood, Sunday School was held in the hall, with the youngest pupils up in the balcony, progressively older groups downstairs and on the stage. Miss Walrond was the superintendent: a middle-aged lady who wore pince nez and nursed a secret affection for the Vicar, as did so many of the Old Girls. She was a leading light in all fundraising enterprises, her name frequently cropping up in PCC minutes. Bazaars were her speciality, which she'd organise at the drop of a hat for such worthy causes as the Organ Fund and the Vicarage. The syllabus was based on a handbook which followed the church's year, but I don't think many of the teachers stuck to it – apart from Bert Hoile, one of those earnest, honest young men belonging to a now vanishing breed. A couple of us once helped him vacuum clean every hassock in the church; a prodigious undertaking and most dusty. The good man's treat was a trip on the Brighton Belle. He was delighted with his success after somebody put a foreign coin in the Sunday collection and he took it to Cook's for an exchange which was in the church's favour. When he became superintendent of the Sunday School, he treated the teachers to a night at the pictures. The film was some Hollywood Biblical epic with the usual indispensable sexy scenes during which, Mary Coombs told me afterwards, Bert squirmed uncomfortably in his seat. The poor man was rather fond of Mary, and once presented her with a bouquet of flowers. Alas, she was not for him; she later married a policeman. Bert, in turn, married Miss Skyrme, a lady of mature years, probably resigned to spinsterhood. Bert's brother Reginald was another teacher at the Sunday School, but he took life far less seriously. He served in the war as a fighter pilot. When the Vicar mentioned his Palestine holiday from the pulpit I used to catch Reginald's eye and will him to laugh because the Palestine holiday was a recurrent theme in the Vicar's sermons. His opening was always 'When I was privileged to visit the Holy Land … ' and my guess is that his holiday treat was paid for by one of the parishioners. Reginald married another Sunday School teacher, Lily Jarman.

Regular attendance at Sunday School was encouraged by means of a weekly stamp, stuck in a little book and a prize was awarded for the neatest, and most complete. This I never received, not because of poor attendance but because I couldn't always be bothered to stick in the stamps. Those I did were crooked. Half-way through the afternoon the children left the hall and went round the corner to the church in Burlington Street for a service of hymns, prayers and a short address by the Vicar. Pupils who were also choirboys changed into cassocks and surplices and sat in the chancel, later occupying the front pew during the address. The lady organist for the children's service was Miss Cooper, daughter of the first incumbent, and we once incurred the frustrated wrath of the poor lady when singing the traditional tune to *All Things Bright and Beautiful.* We la la la'd the descending phrase which follows the second line; and if you know the melody I think you'll agree that the temptation to do this is almost irresistible. She cried out for us to desist, but we knew she was helplessly confined to the organ bench. The *Magnificat* we always sang to the same chant and when I hear it today I am reminded of my mother's Sunday teatime fruit cake. *Loving Shepherd of Thy Sheep* was also usually sung.

Although the facilities were there, I can't recall any full-length play put on by amateurs in the hall. Many years later in the 50s I directed Tom Robinson's *Caste* there, an experience I would rather forget. The scenery got stuck, and the curtain remained down for such a seemingly interminable period that the Vicar sent round a note asking when I proposed to raise it. In the 30s there was once some sort of musical gallimaufry presented by a Mrs Rivett-Drake, whose august name seems appropriate for an organising lady of the church. The show was completely formless with an occasional song; and the programme, typed on wallpaper informed us that the action took place in the village hall of Little Muddlecome – or some such place. Bert Lelliot the local builder, dressed in some sort of Cranford get-up sang *In the Gloaming* which, for some reason, my mother remembered with amusement for years afterwards. The surprise event was a retinue of performers, led by Mrs Rivett-Drake sporting a lorgnette and dressed as Johnny Walker, coming in the main door, chattering noisily, seemingly indifferent to the actors on the stage. The interruption was very welcome; but the evening's entertainment did not improve as a result.

The regular event on a Wednesday evening was a performance by the King's Cliff Light Orchestra conducted by G H Witcombe, admission free with a bowl at the door. Even to my unsophisticated ear they never seemed to play quite in tune, reminding one of an ancient, creaky equipage, drawn by a decrepit nag, stopping and starting in fits and starts but getting there in the end. Somehow. 'We shall now attempt a Haydn symphony' announced Mr Witcombe. They got through the opening bars then seemed to go to pieces. The conductor turned to the audience and laughed. They started again and I believe they did get to the end without serious mishap. The King's Cliff Light Orchestra often performed in church concerts when the Vicar charitably described them as 'first rate'. Other items in those concerts included a Mr Arthur Hyman, the hairdresser in Duke Street, whose jokes never varied. He would read out a letter supposedly from a critic which ran: 'Dear Sir, most of your jokes I have heard before, and the others I haven't heard yet…'. He would look puzzled, then vexed and hastily stuff the missive in his pocket. I've always wondered about that particular joke. Does the punch line really mean anything?

Another of his jokes was about the vicar who turned over two pages when reading the lesson, with comic effect. The Old Girls would look along the row at Canon James to see if he was amused before they dare laugh at something nearly blasphemous. His other joke was about children left to their own devices while their parents went to a dinner party. Mother asked them afterwards how they had passed the time. 'Well, we looked up all the people in the telephone directory called Smellie. When they answered we asked "Are you Smellie?" and when they said "Yes" we asked them what they were going to do about it.' Another artiste was a dear old, bald-headed chap who mimed somebody being attacked by an angry wasp. Not quite a mime, because he used to make a zizzing sound. He used to flap his handkerchief to drive the wasp away. I've seen worse on the professional stage. He also did a street crier calling 'watercress' approaching, and dying away in the distance. For one concert, Tozzer Witcombe wrote a whistling song for the choirboys. On the great day we stood in a nervous line on the stage, scrubbed knees a tremble and dressed in our best bib and tuckers. I can't remember if there were any words, but it was quite a catchy little tune. Tozzer wrote the school song *Onwards and Upwards* for York Place, which later became Varndean, but sadly, I doubt whether it will ever be sung again. Tozzer claimed proudly that Old Vardeanians, in distant parts of the far-flung empire met up again and renewed their friendship after hearing one of them singing the school song. Three choirmen, Handley, Rogers and Langley, alto, tenor and bass respectively sang comic songs about a singularly inept do-it-yourself pater familias: *When Father papered the*

Tozzer's catchy little 'whistling' tune

parlour and *When Father laid the carpet on the stairs*. Annie, one of the Vicar's two servants used to put on fairy musicals in the hall, she and Jennie making all the costumes, which were kept in a big old wardrobe at the top of the vicarage. Annie once appeared in the part of an irate father, appearing at the Tudor window under which his daughter had been serenaded by an unwelcome suitor and throwing down a bag of money. Rather unfortunately, I remember, the disappointed swain was cross-eyed.

Shrove Tuesday Social was probably the highlight of the year. This traditional event began in 1928 at the request of the congregation. At the January meeting of the PCC the Vicar said 'that as people were asking for a Parish Social he would be glad if the ladies present would see to this'. Of course they would. I remember the impatience of the choirboys one Shrove Tuesday when Tozzer kept us practising in the church. 'Nothing much happens to start with', he assured us. We weren't convinced. The varnished deal chairs were placed round the walls to leave a space for the games which included Gentlemen's Hat Trimming. The contestants were given a lady's hat each and could help themselves from a box of ribbons, feathers and other decorations. The competitors then donned their creations and paraded round the hall for the judges' decision. Plates of cakes were, of course, in happy abundance, soon polished off by the choirboys. Tea and coffee were of the urn variety, but nobody complained because those days people weren't so fussy: and anyway, with tickets at only six old pence, refreshments were a bargain. During the break Bimbo, the Vicar's dog came round the hall wagging his tail and receiving a pat from the parishioners. Well, of course he knew them all by smell because the Vicar took Bimbo round with him; and the dog had perfected his master's technique of making a fuss of each person but not lingering too long. We had musical chairs of course, and the usual team games; and by imperishable custom the evening included the Vicar's version of Cock Robin. He always included a verse he'd written himself, different each year. Then *Old Lang Syne* and home. Through the sophisticated eyes of the 1990s all this would seem very tame, but from a distance of over sixty years I look back wistfully and regretfully at times which will never come again.

Money-raising fetes and bazaars – what is the difference? – were regular features in the hall: when has a church not been in need of repainting, repointing or repair? In medieval times the parson held church ales for the same purpose: a parochial booze up with a blessing. Church boilers always seem past their prime and in need of immediate replacement. Heating a church is an expensive business – heating a cathedral a financial nightmare. I don't think I can remember a time from the 30s onwards when the heating system of St Anne's was not in imminent need of repair or replacement. The Fiery Furnace Fete was a great success and parishioners were assured against a chilly church for a year or two.

As church cleaner, my mother was the obvious choice for hall functions when refreshments were provided. She invariably wore a hat for the occasion, even though her duties were confined to the Devil's Kitchen. She used a large galvanised bath for washing up, and I remember the coffee boiling away on the gas ring. Young Barnard, whose father kept the wireless shop in St George's Road, used to organise dances, and I remember him tasting my mother's coffee and pronouncing: 'This is the stuff to give the troops.' The plaintive strains of the saxophone could be heard overhead and the rumble of the trudging feet of the fox-trotters. My mother always managed to spirit away a few cakes for later, domestic consumption, and there were many going spare after the refreshment interval. On one hall function, one of the Old Girls returned a plate after my mother had washed it up and complained that it wasn't clean. 'Let her do it herself' said my mother testily. I don't know how much they paid her for washing up and coffee brewing but I suspect it wasn't much. 'Mrs Packham will do it' was something of a slogan in Kemp Town, and whatever it was, she always did it with a smile.

Mothers' Union Meetings were held in the hall, and once my mother took me with her. Strong on morality, and with rules those days which would have excluded many present day members, I suppose you might describe them as early Women's Libbers. At the meeting I attended I remember a woman giving a talk about immorality on the stage. Her concluding remarks, to enthusiastic applause were 'and the Vicar will stop women undressing on the stage'. How he was to do this was not clear. Did he intend to rush on from the wings with a folding screen and hustle the half-clad woman off the stage or just write 'disgusted' letters to *The Times*? He'd have his time cut out today, fighting an already lost battle.

There was of course a Christmas party held in the hall, and the presents were hung on a large Christmas tree, presented by the Royal Crescent Hotel after their celebrations were over. My mother got a present for being the church cleaner. Young Walter Collyer, recently admitted to the Men's choir was summoned to the platform to receive a present, which occasioned him much embarrassment, and amusement for the other boys: a little furry horse and cart. Who chose the presents that year I don't know, but the poor lad was covered in blushes and confusion.

The Men's Clubroom was a largish room above the main entrance. Membership was confined originally to communicants of the church, but this was later more honoured in the breach than the observance. I can remember a yellowing photograph of the original members, many sporting the obligatory walrus moustaches of the period. Local tradesmen were members among whom were Lelliot the Builder, Chatfield the Watchmaker and several shopkeepers. Kemp Town those days was like a small, self-contained village with the hall in the epicentre.

During the Second World War the hall was rented out to the Education Committee for overflow classes, and every Saturday my mother and I scrubbed the floor.

Picture overleaf: Magnificent altarpiece by Farmer and Brindley, carved out of a solid block of stone. Destroyed during demolition.

In the Beginning

The two Wagners were a dominating influence in Victorian church life. Henry was Vicar of Brighton from 1824 to 1870 and his son Arthur was curate, and later Vicar of St Paul's in West Street, They came of a wealthy family, and Arthur was a liberal benefactor to the Brighton poor. When his father began his ministry, Brighton was already a fashionable resort centred round the Prince Regent's seaside estate, The Royal Pavilion. During the next thirty years the town expanded at an accelerated rate, especially after Brighton was linked by rail with London in 1841. The two parish churches of St Nicholas and the newly built St Peter's could not accommodate the burgeoning population, even with the addition of the two 'overflow' chapels Royal and St James.

As High Churchmen the two Wagners regarded the dissenting chapels mushrooming everywhere in the town with dismay, more especially as these, unlike the Anglican churches, did not charge a pew rent; so they encouraged and funded the building of churches with ample free seating.

One of these was St Anne's in Burlington Street costing £6964.15.11 to which Henry Wagner contributed £2000. The church seated 900 of which 508 seats were free: the others were rented. Recognising this demand, it was not unusual for speculative builders to erect a church for a vicar and his sponsors who then 'auctioned off' the pews. Seemingly there were few bidders for those at St Anne's, and despite the donation of £2000 by the first incumbent, the Reverend Alfred Cooper, the church was burdened with debts for several years to come. Not surprisingly there had been few applicants and many of the clergymen who had made enquiries were quickly put off by the financial liabilities involved. Nearly fifty years later when the Reverend T J James was appointed, there was the same reluctance to take on a church still in debt. St Anne's was built in memory of the Reverend James Churchill Cooke by his mother Maria, whose endowment produced an annual income of £167.13.4, and a further bequest from Mrs Cooke's sister increased the amount to £196.14.11. However, the Reverend Alfred Cooper left most of this untouched, generously allowing the money to accrue for his successor's benefit.

St Anne's was the seventh church built by Cheeseman and Co., who seemed to enjoy the patronage of Henry Wagner, and at the consecration in 1863 he congratulated the firm on the speed in which they had completed the work — a few days over the year. Perhaps they should have taken a little more time and given a little more thought because it was found, many years later, that the Kentish Ragstone had been laid the wrong way, allowing water seepage. I remember how the outside walls used to flake. By the 1860s the classical style had gone out of fashion, and the Gothic, favoured by Augustus Welby Pugin had become popular; and his favourite pupil, Benjamin Ferrey, chose Early Decorated for St Anne's. The church was well proportioned and would have been dwarfed by Wagner's vast showpiece, St Bartholomew's, within which you are silenced by religious awe. By contrast, St Anne's possessed a quiet, motherly reassurance; it was a place to sit and reflect quietly with more of the atmosphere of St John 21 than the Miltonic resonances of Revelation. The magnificent altarpiece depicting the Last Supper was carved out of a solid block of stone weighing over two tons by Farmer and Brindley. The floral carvings of the pillar capitals were a delight: oak, ivy, bramble, hop and vine, Indian and Egyptian water lilies. Money seems to have run out because one or two of the capitals were in block awaiting the sculptor's chisel.

Besides financial worries, the first incumbent was beset with the problem of siting his church; and there seems to have been some acrimonious argument about where this should be. Mrs Cooke wanted the church to be built in the neighbourhood, and certainly Burlington Street isn't far from Charlotte Street where she lived. This did not meet with the unified approval of all the interested parties. Certainly Mrs Cooke had posed a problem because St Mary's had been established in the neighbourhood from 1827 with St George's on the other side, built about the same time. Between the two was a very deprived area whose inhabitants were in no position to pay pew rent. Henry Wagner had met this problem to the north, in Eastern Road, by building All Souls' Church consecrated by the Bishop of Chichester in 1834. Complying with Wagner's policy, nearly all the 1000 seats were free. It would appear, then, that the neighbourhood was already pretty well endowed with Anglican churches: so where should they put St Anne's? Finally it was agreed, with considerable opposition, to build the church in a turning off the sea front, Burlington Street.

As the next incumbent was to discover, the immediate neighbourhood of St Anne's consisted of boarding houses, a case of 'No Continuing City'. In the district served by St Anne's there was a population of between 3000 and 4000 poor, so the church ran a coal club, a lending library, a savings bank, mothers' meetings, a sewing class for girls, a night school for men and boys and – when and if funds could be raised – a cookery class to provide for the sick during the winter. Where all these activities took place is not clear for at this time there was no church hall.

It is remarkable that a church funded in part by High Churchman Wagner in whose gift, presumably, the incumbency lay, should be so anti-ritualistic. Alfred Cooper was a moderate churchman, very staunchly opposed to vestments and the confessional. Through the local press, and probably from the pulpit he argued vehemently against Anglo-Catholicism. Henry Wagner's high praise for a man who could well have been a thorn in his side reveals the generosity of his nature and also his esteem for the Reverend Alfred Cooper.

An early photograph of the interior shows a curtained recess on the left of the chancel, facing the East window, from which the choir processed. Later this would be filled by a Willis Organ, until which time they would have to make do with a harmonium which the Vicar's wife played 'with singular skill and correctness'. A contemporary report states that the choir was not large, 'but it appears to be remarkably well trained and sings well together with good expression' - credit again being accorded to Mrs Cooper. The organ was eventually installed in the 70s and cost about £800 and of course required manual blowing. It was a fine instrument built by Father Willis.

There is a faded photograph of the Reverend Alfred Cooper, which hangs in St George's vestry. He is shown in profile with mutton chop whiskers and has a kindly face. I have the impression that he was a man of firm principle, energetic until his health failed in later years, and certainly generous. He graduated at St John's College, Oxford, and was ordained in 1846, serving for thirteen years as curate at Ryde Parish Church. For a time he was curate at St Nicholas, Brighton where he obviously made a good impression on the Vicar of Brighton, Henry Wagner.

The Reverend Thomas Joseph James, MC, O St J, MA

...or Jumbo as he was known to us choirboys, and Jimmy James to the soldiers who served in the Great War. He studied at Christ's College, Cambridge, graduating in 1898 and obtaining – I assume automatically – his MA in 1903. He told me that he wanted to be a doctor; but he must have undergone a Pauline conversion because in 1899 he took holy orders. He had a bit of luck – or was it Divine Intervention? – with his Greek exam. The night before his finals he pointed to an extract and told his fellow undergraduates: 'That's the passage they'll give us.' And they did.

From what I knew of him in his middle and late years, he must have been a tough cookie in his youth, physically fearless and full of drive. In his eighties when on his way to a bowls tournament at Queen's Park, Brighton he made a grab for a 'bus and missed, landing upon his face. The matron of the Royal Sussex met him, bruised and bleeding and ordered him immediately to hospital. Patched but unbowed he afterwards made his resolute way up to the park and played his game of bowls.

He joined the clergy of the Parish Church of St Peter, Brighton in 1902 where, by the by, he married my parents. In 1909 when senior curate, actively involved in the St Wilfrid's Mission he was appointed to St Anne's in Burlington Street, Brighton. The *Brighton Herald* played Job's comforter:

'One hardly knows at first whether to congratulate Mr James or not on his new appointment. It must place him in a position akin to that of a knight of the time of chivalry who, having achieved one difficult exploit, was rewarded by being set to achieve one still more difficult.'

The report encouragingly concludes:

St Anne's has developed into a backwater, which the moving current of Church life in Brighton has passed by undisturbed. Mr James will go to a church with no congregation, and no district, with no vicarage, with nothing of the many things that are regarded as essential to the proper conduct of a church, and with very little income. The retiring Vicar is about ninety years of age.

From the outset the church needed repairs costing £700. Fund raising then, would be the name of the game for several years to come.

For the first twenty years of his ministry at St Anne's, Jumbo lived in rented accommodation; and it wasn't until well after the Great War that 3, College Road became the official Vicarage. Jumbo postponed the purchase of suitable premises expecting property to become cheaper. Of course it seldom does; and on a much later occasion he delayed repairs to the church roof for the same misguided reason. The house in College Road was finally purchased for £1500, the Ecclesiastical Commissioners contributing £700 upon condition that the parish match it with an equal sum. The Parochial Church Council asked for a further £300 from the

Commissioners to cover legal expenses, survey fees, repairs and decoration.

College Road, then as now, consisted of solidly built mid-Victorian houses with gardens at the back; and for Annie and Jennie, Jumbo's two servants, it must have been an awkward place with the kitchen in the basement and three flights of stairs. But Victorian houses were never built for the convenience of the domestics.

Jumbo met the challenge of an ailing parish with vigour and enthusiasm, and the years before the Great War were not easy. The church was still heavily in debt, and he soon discovered that the parish was not wealthy. Nine tenths was composed of boarding houses with a transient population owing no loyalty to the church. Marine Parade and the Royal Crescent may have had wealthy occupants, as did Portland Place, Sussex Square and Lewes Crescent; but there were several other churches in the locality. St George's, just up the road enjoyed the reputation of being late Regency, and was built in 1824 as the Parish Church of Kemp Town, then regarded as separate from Brighton proper. Jumbo never liked this church; and over forty years later when churches were being 'regrouped' to meet falling congregations, he spoke disparagingly of the building. Bishop Crotty was in the chair, and Jumbo was fighting his corner for the survival of St Anne's. He quoted from a guidebook describing St George's as 'a very good example of a very bad architectural style'. He suggested that it be moved 'brick by brick' to a more suitable site. Heaven alone knows what the good man would have said when in 1986 his beloved church of St Anne's was demolished and the congregation joined St George's. There were also St Mary's in Rock Gardens, St Mark's at the other end of the district, St John the Baptist, RC in Bristol Road and a Methodist Church just across the road. It would take some energetic evangelism – or should we call it 'poaching'? – to win back parishioners who had forsaken St Anne's during the declining years of the Reverend Alfred Cooper.

But Jumbo was energetic and had charm in full measure, so can we blame him for using this to woo the wealthy? This has always been a function of a priest, and even those robust young ministers of strong Leftist persuasion who take on tough parishes in deprived areas shove the begging bowl under the noses of the rich. Many years after Jumbo died, one of his successors, the Reverend Ray Newham enjoyed the patronage of Mrs Miller, widow of the comedian Max Miller, who lived in Burlington Street; and his blue jokes paid for the blue carpeting round the altar.

Jumbo won his MC (Military Cross) in the Great War, and he cut a good figure in his army chaplain's uniform. There was a photograph hanging in the church hall. It is hardly surprising, then, that he was surrounded by admiring ladies of the parish. I remember his being smothered by clucking old hens at a little railway station: what a flutter and a fuss they made of him as he stepped out of the carriage!

He loved to name-drop from the pulpit and in the parish magazine, serving the dual purpose of buttering up the richer and more influential among his congregation while impressing the humbler parisioners. Lady Florence Baddeley, JP had frequent mentions, as did Sir Hubert Bond, KBE, DSc, MD Edin. FRCP London; while a smattering of double barrels, Mrs D'Arcy Carden, Miss R Guinness-Sharpe and

Mrs Drummond-Roberts improved the general tone.

But he also had time for the humbler parishioners, and would use his influence when youngsters were applying for jobs – or getting them out of scrapes. His writ ran wide in Brighton when a reference from the Vicar was an almost indispensable document. He found jobs for my mother, but I suspect with mixed motives: he may have been doing her a favour but also earning the gratitude of the Old Girls. Perhaps I do him an injustice. He once found an odd job for me. 'Would you like to earn thruppence?' he boomed. My task was to pick up twigs in the vicarage garden, which didn't take long, nor was it very taxing. Looking back I think it was a disguised tip.

As son of the church cleaner I always felt somewhat below the salt, and certainly Jumbo was inclined to discriminate between his wealthier parishioners and the others. On two occasions my mother was made to feel an inferior. The gratings over the heating pipes had been removed and my mother cleaned out nearly a century of debris. 'Mrs Packham is very disappointed,' Jumbo announced afterwards to the Old Girls. 'She didn't find any money under the gratings.' A joke, of course; but my mother took it badly. On another occasion he stopped her for a chat in the street, and broke off in the middle when he espied a more important parishioner across the road. Well, who has not experienced a similar slight at one of those dreadful stand-up parties, where you hold a cardboard plate in one hand and a wine glass in the other and the person you're chatting to is looking over your shoulder for somebody more important to buttonhole?

Jumbo's stipend was something under £400 per annum until a suggestion was made in 1921 to allocate a pound every Sunday from the collection to make it up into a round £400. 'This met the approval of all present.' As the congregation increased, and the church finances became healthier, the subject of a curate cropped up. In January 1923 Jumbo announced that 'a clergyman was coming the next day to see me respecting a curacy'. Apparently nothing came of this meeting, and anyway, two issues dominated the affairs of St Anne's at this time: The Organ and The Vicarage. By September 1925 there had been no suitable applicants for the post of curate, but the following year the Vicar announced that he had been fortunate in obtaining the services of the Reverend Sidney Thomas. He would do Sunday work, visiting and day services for a salary of £200, which was increased the following year to £250.

'I hate begging for money from the pulpit' was Jumbo's apologetic approach when funds were needed. Perhaps he did, but he was also quite good at it. By 1922 the treasurer presented a very healthy balance sheet, and the Vicar's Easter gift was £87.8s.3d. The number of communicants at that festival was a record 711, so things were obviously looking up at St Anne's.

Until the outbreak of the Second World War, St Anne's went from strength to strength under Jumbo's ministry. The choir became an important feature in church worship, and the music library was probably unequalled in Brighton apart from St Peter's. The magnificent altarpiece depicting the Last Supper was originally plain stone: in the 1930s it was embellished with gold leaf and colour. The Lady Chapel was added, the lighting improved and the fabric of the church was kept in sound condition.

Then, during the morning service on September 3rd, 1939 the verger solemnly made his way up to Jumbo's stall and handed him a note. At the end of the service Jumbo came down to the chancel gate and announced that war had been declared. 'I have offered my services as chaplain' he told the congregation, 'but they tell me I am too old. So my place will be with you.' The outbreak of the Second World War was a punctuation mark. Young men from the choir were killed, Kemp Town was bombed and attitudes changed. We saw 1945 through different eyes, and the peaceful period between the two wars was a lost world. Jumbo, now past his prime, soldiered on for another ten years, adding another verse to *Cock Robin* every Shrove Tuesday and regretting the passing of the Old Brigade in the parish. I shall remember him sitting up in bed wearing striped flannel pyjamas smiling sadly. 'Almost every day I see the name of a friend in the obituary column of the *Telegraph*' he said.

The East Window and Chancel

Change and Decay

'… in all around I see.' When we sang that hymn in the 30s Jumbo never imagined this would apply to his parish. After the retirement of the previous incumbent, whose congregation had dwindled to a mere handful, Jumbo had put his heart and soul into resurrecting a dead parish. He had succeeded, and St Anne's had become his world, his delight and his very reason for living. By the time he had sung his last Cock Robin verse at the Shrove Tuesday social, Canon James was an old man with failing faculties, grappling with the problems of a changing parish. He played his last card at one PCC meeting. Mrs Lynn, the policeman's wife in charge of the church linen, complained it was falling apart and beyond repair. In his prime, Jumbo would have given a quick rejoinder; he had a way of overruling proposals which he considered against the interests of the church. This time, however, he used a different ploy. 'If it is felt that I am no longer capable as a vicar of this parish, and that it is time for me to go …' he began, reducing Mrs Lynn to tears. Up leapt one of the Old Guard, his loyal Vicar's Warden Mr Forward to assure the Vicar of our full support, and that it would be his decision, and his alone when to retire. But what would the Canon think of Kemp Town in 1998?

Here he comes, bouncing down the vicarage steps in College Road, confident of being greeted by two out of every three people. Today, alas, he'll be disappointed because nobody will even recognise him: all the Old Girls have passed across to that Further Shore, where they may polish, arrange flowers and tidy hymn books to a blissful Eternity: their tins of Bluebell producing an even brighter, extra-terrestrial shine, and their lilies will never fade. Perhaps he'll call in at Lelliot's the Builders and have a word with Bert about a repair job in the church, remembering that a timely compliment about his solo last Sunday might soften the bill. But what's this? New, ornamental gates across the yard entrance with a strange digital locking device? No good rattling the gates: they won't open unless you know the combination. Peering through he sees the cobbled frontage of the old workshop converted into Highly Desirable Flatlets. The covered-in ladder rack down the side of the yard is gone, and not a barrow in sight. He isn't to know that Lelliot's have long since been absorbed into Braybons the Builders.

Then he remembers some church business with Lloyd's Bank on the corner of College Road, and is reassured to find the outside of the building unchanged. He decides to have a chat with Mr Lawson the manager, confident that no appointment is ever necessary for the Vicar. There are few places, in fact, including the Town Hall, where he could not just drop in unannounced. But Mr Lawson is no longer in the land of the living having mercifully been spared all the paraphernalia of electronic accountancy. All the clerks seem to have been replaced by women. The solid mahogany counters and leather chairs have gone, and why are they all sitting behind thick glass screens? Heads are shaken with sad smiles at his questions, so bewildered, he leaves.

Outside he is astonished to find people slipping shiny cards into a little slot and receiving wads of notes. Ordinary people, too: hardly the sort to have a bank account. But there they are, pulling out small fortunes in fivers and tenners. An unwashed, unshaven and malodorous man in his thirties takes him by the arm. 'I haven't eaten for a week, Father,' he mutters. 'Could you help me out?' From the fastness of the vicarage, the Canon is accustomed to dealing with vagrants. He has an arrangement with Captain Pounds of the Church Army in Upper St James' Street. Instead of money which, says the Canon, they will only spend on drink, he gives them a meal ticket. He offers one to the beggar, who swears horribly, shakes a fist and tells him what he can do with his meal ticket. The Canon is not to know that the man's pressing need is not even drink - but a fix, which is expensive.

Something is going on in St Anne's Hall across the road: is young Barnard from the wireless shop getting ready for another dance? And what, in heaven's name is that strange sign over the doors - 'Kemp Town Pier'? Why Pier? Ever more confused he enters and finds a variety of stalls selling everything from new laid eggs to second hand junk. A jumble sale with a difference. Mrs Baker never mentioned it, and she certainly didn't put a notice in the parish magazine. And wait a minute! Where has my photograph gone - the one of me in army chaplain's uniform? And they've taken down the two large pictures of Eliza and John Nixon. Was that discussed and approved at the last PCC meeting? The place looks shabby and uncared for. He'll have a word with Mr Christian about it; perhaps he'll catch him coming out of the 'chemist's shop'.

Then he overhears a snatch of conversation: 'I hear they're turning the hall into flats.' Her friend nods and tells her that the locals are up in arms over the plan. 'Well, who wants that sort of person living in the neighbourhood? It'll lower the tone of the place.'

Turn St Anne's Hall into flats? No - that can't be true. He'll call an extraordinary meeting of the PCC immediately. Flats! It's unthinkable. Confused and angry he leaves the hall and decides to have a word with Chatfield the Watchmaker. Perhaps he's heard something. But the shop is gone. Well, no, the shop's still there but with another sign over the window. So where's Mr Chatfield with his neatly trimmed Cardinal Richlieu moustache? Brampton's the Butcher's is still on the corner of Burlington Street although the frontage looks different somehow. Something is missing. The iron rail above the windows is still there and he remembers it before the Great War, hung with carcasses or at Christmas time, fat, plucked geese with a ruffle of feathers. Ah, then he sees what's missing! The Coat of Arms. By appointment to the late King Edward the Seventh. He wonders why they've taken it down and decides to pop into Evershed the grocers on the opposite corner. Old Evershed will know what's going on in Kemp Town if anybody does. But wait a minute. An off licence? He looks above the window to make sure but there is no question about it. Unwins. He'll have to sit down quietly and think things out. He has had a very puzzling, not to say distressing morning so far. He reaches in his pocket for the vestry key and then receives the biggest shock of all. The church is gone. Instead of grey stone walls and a row of Gothic windows he is confronted by a block of flats.

* * * * *

Canon James was mercifully spared from seeing the destruction of his church. For some months in the 1980s services alternated between St Anne's and St George's. There was much discussion during this transitional period on both a diocesan and parochial level, but it became increasingly clear that St Anne's would have to go. St George's was a listed building, Late Regency, with associations of royalty and interesting features like the fishermen's gallery and the Peel vaults. Letters were sent to the Church Commissioners and to the local press protesting about the demolition of St Anne's but it was like throwing a feather against a force nine gale. I quote from a letter I received from the Church Commissioners: 'St Anne's Church, which is not listed under the Town and Country Planning Acts as a building of special architectural or historic interest, was declared redundant by a pastoral scheme on 1 July 1983.'

And more damning still: '... the building was of such small historic or architectural interest that its demolition would not in their opinion be objectionable on that ground.'

Alternative use for St Anne's was sought, and at one time the Brighton Greek Orthodox Church showed an interest in the building, but later decided on Windsor Lodge in the High Street. And so, as the *Argus* put it in January 1984 'Surprise plans to knock down a Brighton church have stunned worshippers.'; and in February 1986 demolition actually began. Some few things were saved from destruction including the Lady Chapel, which was removed in a cloak and dagger operation under cover of darkness to St Bartholomew's Church, where it now stands in a side alcove. The iron chancel gate went to All Saints' Church, Hove, and some windows and a marble pavement to a restored church at Portsmouth. Two windows went to the New Chapel for the Deaf Association in Carlton Hill and an altar to Pevensey Church. But the most wanton act of vandalism was the destruction of the altarpiece of the Last Supper, carved out of a solid block of stone.

I suppose the word 'desecration' is inappropriate when a church has been de-consecrated. But when I entered the building during the demolition, I could think of no other term to describe what was taking place. A bonfire had been lit in the nave, the floorboards had been ripped up and a great pile of broken woodwork awaited the flames in the chancel. Beneath the bare joists were broad, curled up wood shavings, just as they had fallen from the carpenters' jackplanes in the 1860s. In the flickering light of the fire I was watching the destruction of a building in which I had been christened, confirmed and married. My children Simon and Francesca were also christened here and sang in the choir with me. Standing in the middle of it all with her mop and bucket, I wonder what my mother would have made of it all.

Postscript
Kemp Town Village,
1930

In the immediate vicinity of St Anne's was a range of shops from which most human wants could be supplied. At one end of the spectrum was Miss Hagger's Day Nursery in Bristol Road where I was once planted as an unwilling and very tearful toddler; and even at that tender age I was aware of the prevailing odour of wet knickers. At the other end was Prior the Undertaker, situated conveniently near the church. In that same road were two hairdressers, father and son, two shoe shops, two or three bakers, greengrocers, butchers, radio shops, several pubs and two building firms. Many of these supported the church magazine with advertisements, but for which I doubt whether it would have paid its way. 'Will readers kindly mention this magazine when patronising shops advertised?' was the request. Like many church magazines of that time, it was a singularly dull publication with the usual notices of births, marriages and deaths, socials and church outings. It missed a coup many years later when my old choirboy friend Derek Stenning was reading anthropology at Cambridge. He was sent on an expedition to some remote caves in the Sahara there to study primitive wall paintings. Jumbo, himself a Cambridge man, invited Derek to write a series of articles for the church magazine, which he did. 'But Maurice,' he told me afterwards,

'I had to leave out the best bits.' Apparently those paintings left nothing to the imagination. Well, I suppose it might have shocked the Old Girls.

Lelliot and Sons the builders and decorators had premises in College Road not far from the vicarage, and a shop on St George's Road. Bert Lelliot, the senior partner, sang in the choir no doubt casting an occasional eye over all the damp places, crumbling brickwork and pews in need of re-varnishing, and totting up a rough estimate in his head. My brother George, who left Park Street School at fourteen, began his career at Lelliot's, pushing a barrow and learning his trade of electrician from 'Lobby', Bert's younger brother. George had a moment of face burning embarrassment when the Canon's voice boomed across the road one day. 'Packham! Why were you not at Bible Class on Sunday?' His workmates teased him unmercifully afterwards, and I think this may have been the incident which put him off church for good. He was an incorrigible practical joker, and once rigged up a device in the workshop loo involving a metal plate, wires and a battery. Passing water became an electrifying and unforgettable experience as one of his workmates later told me. When war broke out in 1939 he connected a microphone to the radio in the shed where the men ate their sandwiches, concealing himself, and then announcing in the best Stewart Hibbert tones that the entire British Fleet had been sunk. A year or two later George was dangerously wounded in the famous Malta Convoy. He was very badly burnt, peppered with shrapnel that emerged occasionally years later, and he lost a finger. In 1938, just before Hitler invaded Czechoslovakia he and Lobby were rewiring a hotel on the front. Pride of place would go to a large chandelier from abroad, which they unpacked carefully and laid on the floor. Lobby must have had his mind on other things because he walked through the door smoking his accustomed pipe and crunched over the chandelier. This had come from Czechoslovakia and there would be no replacements from that country for many a long year.

Kenneth Lonsdale was the classroom clown and his father ran the confectioners and newsagents in St George's Road. One day Miss Dawson, for whom I nursed a deep but secret affection, decided to take the wind out of Kenneth's sails. 'Hands up all those who think Kenneth Lonsdale is a very silly boy.' With misguided loyalty I kept mine folded, but every other hand shot up. 'But Maurice Packham' she added, 'is ten times sillier than Kenneth Lonsdale.' His mocking laugh made me realise that my sympathy was undeserved. Some time later he told me that his father wanted a word with me. A free handout of sweets, I hoped. But alas, no. 'Are you the boy that makes my Kenneth misbehave at school?' demanded his father. I was astounded by this accusation for the boot was surely on the other foot, but held my peace while being matted.

Evershed and Marsh on the corner of Burlington Street was one of those old established grocers who sold everything in the comestible line: wines, spirits, beers, candied fruit, and biscuits out of square tins arranged in front of the counter. The mingled smells were a delight which no present day supermarket could emulate. I said the biscuit tins were square but, of course, they were really slightly rectangular for a very good reason that was once explained to me, but which I have forgotten. When my Aunt Cissy came on a visit from Littlehampton she bought Uncle Charlie's special black pepper from Evershed and Marsh: apparently a rarity which wasn't generally available. Old Marsh wore a brown overall coat when serving behind the counter, had a walrus moustache – white as I remember – and a manner to match. His wife was nicknamed Queen Mary by the Old Girls because she made her way down Burlington Street with regal dignity and wore a toque like the queen's.

The 'chemist shop' or *Burlington* was an Edlin's house those days and there were many others in the town, all with different and sometimes exotic decors. One was Spanish Colonial; but the jewel in the crown was *The King and Queen* in Marlborough Place in splendid mock Tudor. I remember an American GI in the war taking a photograph of what he thought was little old England, perhaps not noticing the date on the drainpipe: 1934. However, *The Burlington* was in good old traditional style providing a welcome haven for my mother to enjoy her Guinness and a hidey-hole for the verger, Mr Christian. Long before pub meals became almost obligatory, *The Golden Cannon* a few doors along St George's Road provided cooked meat meals at the bar; and almost cheek by jowl with the church hall was *The Northumberland Arms*, another watering hole for thirsty vergers. *The Barley Mow* was a little further on and probably unaltered since it was built.

William Stead on the corner of Bloomsbury Place claimed to be complete house furnishers and I remember buying a second hand piano there just after the last war. It was German, with a good action and tone; but just as I handed over the cash the sales assistant who was a member of St Anne's choir sounded a cautionary note, 'I should mention it has woodworm.' As part of the bargain he gave me a tin of Rentokil – and those were lindane days – but never wished me good hunting. I should say it had woodworm! Riddled with it at the bottom, which I soaked over and over again with the vermicide. Despite my best efforts, however, it spread through the floorboards and into my mother's china cabinet.

My first port of call on the way to Sunday evening service was Maynard's the confectioners in Bristol Road. 'Buy something to last' was always my mother's advice so I usually settled for Lime Juice Pods at two ounces a penny. Although I couldn't resist the temptation to crunch them rather than reduce them to a sliver by sucking them slowly, you could hide them under your tongue to avoid a ticking off by the choirmaster. Truelock's in Upper Bedford Street sold ha'penny bags of 'broken'. These he dispensed from a tin box. 'Broken' consisted of the remains at the bottom of sweet jars; and in your bag you might have a Montpelier drop, a wine gum or two, boiled sweets and, if you were lucky, a squashed chocolate. Usually your half penn'orth was a coagulated lump resembling a specimen from some remote geological strata. A penny was the usual limit of my expenditure, for which you could even obtain three ounces of liquorice cuttings. Some of the sweet jars in Mr Maynard's shop were shaped like glass urns from which the more expensive confectionery was dispensed: lavender coloured cachous to sweeten the breath, sugared almonds and brown tablets impressed with lettering. It would be difficult to classify the last either as medicinal or confection; but in more recent years the ingredients were changed because the original recipe contained opium. All these delights were quite beyond my modest means, but for a ha'penny you could buy a Bassett's Sherbet Fountain (Beware of Imitations) which I believe can still be obtained today, or a Sherbet Dab which came in a triangular packet with a blob of toffee on a stick to extract the sherbet by spit adhesion.

Quarter day when we choirboys were paid was a time for celebration and a customary visit to Barker's cooked meat shop near Lloyd's Bank. The usual choice was saveloys; and I don't know whether it ever occurred to us that the name of the shop was associated with the colloquial term for sausage.

Near Greenyer's Stores, another all-purpose grocers and hardware suppliers – the name survives still on the wall – was Barnard's Radio and Electrical shop. Young Barnard was a tubby man with glasses who organised dances in the church hall. I also remember him playing a part in a play at the Dorset Gardens Methodist's hall. At my tender age I assumed that the hoarse whispering from the prompt side was part of the performance; but I have since realised that young Barnard had forgotten his lines. From what I can remember, he played an anxious swain trying to persuade the heroine to elope with him on his yacht. Her reluctance and the forgotten lines resulted in a very protracted and inconclusive scene.

There were five butchers, one of which even sported a royal coat of arms. This was Brampton's, purveyors of meats to the late King Edward the Seventh. It would take a stretch of the imagination to visualise Teddy buying his chops over the counter; but it is an historical fact that he stayed for a week in 1908 at 1 Lewes Crescent. To these august doors, then, the butcher's boy from Bramptons made his deliveries. The royal coat of arms remained above the shop on the corner of Burlington Street through five reigns until it was removed some years ago.

And so, as Jumbo proceeded up and down his Kemp Town parish he was generally recognised and greeted rather in the manner of a country squire. He never had a car and travelled by Number Seven 'bus. He sat on a side seat near the door, and somebody once remarked that it was like 'an at home day' when you boarded the 'bus with Jumbo ready with his smile and greeting.

Acknowledgements

A Guide To The Buildings of Brighton. McMillan
Martin
Victorian Churches of Sussex. D Robert Ellerton,
Phillimore
The Encyclopaedia of Brighton. Timothy Carder
Sussex Churches and Chapels, Royal Pavilion Art
Gallery & Museums
Brighton Herald 1909 & 1912
Brighton and Hove Leader, 19.6.98
Evening Argus 25.1.84
Burgess Hill In Old Picture Postcards, Frederick M
Avery, 1988
Photographs, Walter Collyer
Dolphin, Magazine of Varndean Grammar School for
Boys
The Organ Today, Herbert Norman and E J John
Norman
The Organ, William Leslie Sumner
Newspaper cuttings: Brighton Churches 1870-1880
Wolseley Collection, Hove Reference Library

About this book

This book was made by Margaret Bell, Steve Hill, Sheena Macdonald and Anna Lindequist, with the help of John Knight. We would also like to thank Erica Smith and Jack Latimer for sharing their knowledge and Jackie Blackwell and Jane Reid of QueenSpark for their support.

With thanks to Brighton Local Studies Library for the cover photo.

Printed by Digaprint, Hollingdean Road, Brighton.

About QueenSpark Books

QueenSpark is a community writing and publishing group based in Brighton. We believe that everyone has a history and that anyone who wants to can be a writer. Our aim is to encourage and publish writing by people who do not normally get into print. QueenSpark Books is not a commercial company. We have two part-time paid workers, but the rest of us are volunteers. One of our aims is to produce books, gaining and sharing skills and confidence as we go.

We have several active writing workshops in Brighton and Hove. Our manuscripts group reads manuscripts that are sent to us and sets up book-making groups for those we are able to publish. All groups work on a co-operative basis.

QueenSpark Books is a member of the national Federation of Worker Writers and Community Publishers. We can give you the addresses of the other Federation groups.

QueenSpark gratefully acknowledges the support of South East Arts, the local council of Brighton and Hove, and the Foundation for Sports and the Arts.

If you would like more information, or would like to get involved in any of our activities, please contact:

QueenSpark Books
49 Grand Parade
Brighton BN2 2QA
Telephone and Fax: 01273 571710
Email: info@queensparkbooks.org.uk
Website: http://www.queensparkbooks.org.uk